THE STRUCTURALISTS ON MYTH

THEORISTS OF MYTH
(VOL. 6)

GARLAND REFERENCE LIBRARY
OF THE HUMANITIES
(VOL. 1167)

Theorists of Myth
Robert A. Segal, Series Editor

THE STRUCTURALISTS ON MYTH
An Introduction

Roland A. Champagne

GARLAND PUBLISHING, INC. • NEW YORK & LONDON
1992

Library of Congress Cataloging-in-Publication Data

Champagne, Roland A.
   The structuralists on myth : an introduction / by Roland A.
Champagne.
        p.   cm. — (Theorists of myth ; vol. 6) (Garland reference library
of the humanities ; vol. 1167)
   Includes bibliographical references (p.   ) and index.
   ISBN 0-8240-3447-3 (alk. paper)
   1. Structural anthropology—France. 2. Myth—Structural analysis. 3.
Mythology, Classical. 4. Gernet Center (France) I. Title. II. Series.
III. Series: Garland reference library of the humanities ; vol. 1167.
GR161.G425   1992
398.2'0938—dc20   92-22998
                                                                        CIP

Printed on acid-free, 250-year-life paper
Manufactured in the United States of America

DEDICATION

For Nina, who is my model for demythologizing
as she always finds the heart of the story.

CONTENTS

SERIES EDITOR'S FOREWORD

As a theory of myth, not to say of culture as a whole, structuralism peaked in popularity in the late 1960s and early 1970s. It was superseded by one or more varieties of "poststructuralism." While Claude Lévi-Strauss, the key founder of structuralism, continues to write, Jacques Derrida and others have succeeded him as reigning intellectuals of the moment. Still, the impact of structuralism, like that of functionalism and psychoanalysis, will doubtless endure.

While no longer in vogue in anthropological and literary circles, structuralism continues to be employed with even increasing fervor by classicists. It is not merely disparate individuals who have been using the theory but a formal, organized group of French classicists headed by Jean-Pierre Vernant. In 1975 Vernant founded the "Center for Comparative Research on Ancient Societies." The Center was subsequently named the "Gernet Center" in honor of Vernant's influential teacher, Louis Gernet. The most prominent members of the Center, besides Vernant himself, are Marcel Detienne, Pierre Vidal-Naquet, and Nicole Loraux. "Second-generation" members of the Center include François Hartog, Françoise Frontisi-Ducroux, Annie Schnapp-Gourbeillon, François Lissarrague, Laurence Kahn, Jesper Svenbro, Alain Moreau, and Jean-Louis Durand.

The members of the Center have not simply applied but adapted Lévi-Strauss' brand of structuralism. Over the years Lévi-Strauss has regularly been lambasted by critics for isolating myth from its various contexts—social, cultural, political, economic, even sexual. In a famous 1964 essay on the Tsimshian Indian myth of Asdiwal, Lévi-Strauss did provide a detailed ethnographic analysis of a myth. He examined and integrated geographical, economic, sociological, and cosmological factors. Yet thereafter, as before, he largely analyzed myth in the abstract.

Vernant and his fellow classicists at the Gernet Center have sought to tether Lévi-Strauss' structuralism to the more conventional classicist concern with context. Preferring for that reason to label their approach "structural" rather than "structuralist," they have taken Lévi-Strauss' analysis of the Asdiwal myth as their model. They scrutinize myths not only for their internal order, or structure, but at least as much for their external one—for the relationship between a myth and other aspects of classical culture. The relationship may turn out to be causal, functional, or merely symmetrical. The aspect examined may be social, cultural, political, economic, or sexual. As the heirs of Lévi-Strauss, the members of the Center seek to decipher underlying, often latent patterns in the myths they scrutinize, but they then seek to connect those patterns to comparable ones in the culture at large.

Because the context studied is the Greek one, the members of the Center are necessarily particularists rather than, like Lévi-Strauss, universalists. Myths are taken as the expressions of distinctively Greek ideas and practices rather than, as for Lévi-Strauss, manifestations of the working of the human mind per se. The meanings and functions of myths are also seen as evolving—in response, for example, to the rise of the city-state—rather than, as for Lévi-Strauss, fixed.

The Gernet Center scholars are especially concerned with distinguishing written myths, with which they deal, from oral ones, with which Lévi-Strauss deals. Classical myths are those of a literate rather than a nonliterate society. While initially oral, they were written down and are examined in their written versions.

By training a professor of French rather than of classics, Roland Champagne treats the Gernet School as a distinctively French movement. He traces the influences on Vernant of not only Lévi-Strauss but also Roland Barthes, the other pioneering French structuralist. He then traces the influence on Detienne, Vidal-Naquet, and Loraux of Vernant and Lévi-Strauss alike. He also considers the influence on Vernant and in turn on the others of the pre-structuralists Gernet and Ignace Meyerson. Champagne explains the distinctive topics to which each leading member of the Center is devoted. He uses the case of the Oedipus myth to illustrate the distinctive approach of each member. He continually demonstrates how members of the Center modify Lévi-Strauss' approach to suit their individual purposes. At the same time he notes the

x

influences of members on one another. His book provides a most helpful overview of the work to date of French structuralists both in classics and in general.

ACKNOWLEDGMENTS

I am beholden to Nina Ekstein for making time to edit my writing,

To Brian Vandenburg for his discussions and readings about myth over the last ten years,

To Judi Lipsett and Char Miller for their innumerable kindnesses to this wanderer between San Antonio and St. Louis,

To Craig Likness for references that only a true bibliophile and friend could provide,

To Steve Hause for his assistance with historical details,

To Pierre Vidal-Naquet for his assistance with details about the Gernet Center,

To my colleagues at the University of Missouri-St. Louis for their support of my research with a 1990 Chancellor's Humanities Award, and

To Robert Segal for his conception of the project and its focus at various stages in its evolution.

The Structuralists on Myth

Chapter One

THE STRUCTURE OF MYTH

According to the French anthropologist Claude Lévi-Strauss, myths are the products of the resourceful ingenuity (in French, *bricolage*)[1] of indigenous peoples selecting narrative materials from their environments. The nature of this resourceful ingenuity has intrigued a group of French intellectuals during the past thirty years. This group is called "structuralist" because its members attribute the survival, the origin, and the function of myths to common crosscultural factors they identify as "structures." These structures are bundles of information not obvious either to the narrator or to the listener. The bundles are collected features that reveal either the reasons for the survival of myths, or their origins, or their functions within their contexts. The structuralists consider themselves to have talents as the collectors from myths of these bundles of information. The structuralists do not always agree about the application of the word "structuralist" to myth. However, they can be generally classified according to whether they bundle myths by 1) the survival of myth, 2) the origin of myth, or 3) its function within a specified context.

The survival of myth especially interests those concerned with the anthropological and philosophical aspects of myths such as Lévi-Strauss (b. 1906) and Roland Barthes (1915-1980). Those who discuss origins are often linked with philology, which studies the evolution of words in the narratives of myths. Jean-Pierre Vernant (b. 1914), Marcel Detienne (b. 1936), and Nicole Loraux (b. 1943) practice this

1

kind of structuralist analysis of myths. The function of myths
appeals to those seeking to recover the cultural contexts of
myths. Pierre Vidal-Naquet (b. 1930) and sometimes Vernant
take this opportunity.
    Barthes and Lévi-Strauss study the survival of myth in
culture. Lévi-Strauss analyzes the oral folklore of North and
South American Indian tribes to derive insights into how the
"human spirit" (*l'esprit humain*) expresses itself. Barthes
proposes broad formal categories for the survival of cultural
unity in mythologies unconsciously constructed by the routines
of daily life. Lévi-Strauss provides a model of survival known
as ethnographic analysis, which is further developed by the
other two camps. That model is best exemplified in his reading
of the Asdiwal myth.
    The functionalist position of Vernant and Vidal-Naquet
takes the ethnographic method as its model and develops a
social and historical context within which myths provide
meaning. Vernant is the primary exponent of the social
functionalist position. Vidal-Naquet advocates a historical
context. The functionalist approach differs from that of Lévi-
Strauss and Barthes in its emphasis on myth as a source of
meaning for a particular culture rather than as a source of
universal human expression.
    The philological, or etymological, group of French
structuralism explains the roots of a myth and its continuing
meaning as changes or developments of those origins. Detienne
and Loraux (as well as Vernant and Vidal-Naquet
occasionally) use the etymology of Greek words to gain insight
into some of the classical myths. They use the tracing of the
origins of concepts to plot the historical development of myths
along with pertinent concepts such as law, family, and
equality. The philological method is often combined with the
methods of the functionalists in the work of the Gernet
Center, founded by Vernant in the early 1970s.
    The three groups both seek connections within a specific
myth and link groups of myths into common bundles of
meaning. The survivalist view of myth finds connections that
have nothing to do with the historical origins of myths. Both
Lévi-Strauss and Barthes are generally concerned with non-

written, and therefore undocumented, myths. The ties of these myths to their culture are thus not so empirical and verifiable as they are speculative and abstract. By contrast, Vernant, Detienne, and Vidal-Naquet began to understand in the early 1970s that written myths had characteristics unique to their form as literature. Written myths were composed within a specifiable culture, at a specifiable moment, for a specifiable audience, with specifiable components. The connections made by the structural method had to address these distinctive marks of written myths. In some cases, the oral myths could not be studied together with them because of the unique form of written myths.

The Gernet Center was founded as a place where the structural method could be applied to the classics. At this Center, Vernant, Detienne, Vidal-Naquet, and Loraux have developed various examples of the functionalist and the philological structural methods. Before getting into the specifics of the various structuralist presentations of myth, let us look at the reasons for the use of the words "structure" and "structural" within a general theory of myth analysis. I will then provide an overview of the principal contributors of the "structuralist" ideology and of the way their views provide different readings of the Oedipus myth—a subject of much controversy among the French structuralists.

THE STRUCTURALIST THEORY OF MYTH

The word "structure" was borrowed from the discipline of linguistics, where a structure provides a diagram for the binary principles of contradiction residing in the logical explanations of language. For example, the science of pronunciation, phonetics, describes the letter "s" as pronounced in different ways depending on its environment. The opposition of voiced and unvoiced consonants constitutes a phonetic structure that helps to explain the phenomenon by grouping the pronunciation of the letter "s" into a diagram resembling an accountant's balance sheet to reveal what is known in phonology as minimal phonemic pairs. By analyzing the absence or presence of the voiced or unvoiced "s" as a minimal pair in various environments (e.g., between vowels, as part of another syllable), rules can then be constructed about the changes in the pronunciation of the letter "s."

Similarly, Lévi-Strauss finds binary structures to be helpful in studying myth by setting up the parameters of values implied within the myth. By juxtaposing two contradictory factors in a myth such as human and divine intervention, he sets up polar opposites and a semantic line dividing the story into bundles, or clusters, of meanings—for example, according to whether an event represents human or divine intervention. This cluster of meanings is a whole structure which interacts with other structures to compose the system of a given myth.

The very title "structuralist" for the many contributors in this group is confusing in that no single philosophy, methodology, or ideology links them together as a school. In addition to French structuralism, there have been competing "structuralist" schools in the Soviet Union, Czechoslovakia, Switzerland, Denmark, and the United States.[2] The word "structuralism" in France is used to speak about a group of five individuals (Claude Lévi-Strauss, Roland Barthes, Jacques Lacan, Michel Foucault, and Louis Althusser) who from the period 1958 to 1968 were independently involved in bringing the methods of the social sciences to bear on humanistic endeavors. Only Barthes and Lévi-Strauss applied the structuralist attitude to the study of myths.

Barthes was one of the first structuralists to offer a theory of the structure of myths. Barthes (*Mythologies*, 1957) theorizes that myth is "a form ... defined not by the recipient of its message but by the way it expresses the message."[3] Thus he is concerned not with what myth means to listeners (its content) but with how myth expresses its meaning (its form). As a formal entity, myth can be analyzed either structurally— by encompassing universal narrative strategies of how myths are expressed—or textually—by analyzing the rhetoric, diction, and syntax. Barthes chooses to focus on the structural properties of a myth's form.

Barthes was not the first to focus on the form of myths.

During the 1920s and 1930s Russian Formalism, as exemplified by Vladimir Propp in his *The Morphology of Folktales* (1928), had offered a method which identifies the structure of stories as the sequence of recurring motifs. The Formalist research established narrative meaning as an imitation of the structure of a sentence by linking the narrative motifs in the model of subject, predicate, and direct and indirect objects. In addition, the Prague School of linguistics led by Roman Jakobson (1896-1982), the Russian-born phonologist, had investigated the phonetic aspects of language during the 1920s and had advocated the formation of the discipline of structural linguistics. During the early 1940s Jakobson taught Lévi-Strauss this linguistic method. Lévi-Strauss adapted the model to investigate anthropological data such as the myths he had heard while in Brazil during the early 1930s. Lévi-Strauss objected to Propp's exclusion of content, so he adopted the word "structure" from linguistics to provide a concept that would encompass both content and form. Rather than concentrating exclusively on how a story is told (its form), as Propp is alleged to have done with his stringing together motifs, Lévi-Strauss also incorporates what a story has to say (its content). As Lévi-Strauss identified structures among myths from different peoples and disparate geographical and historical backgrounds, he began to maintain that the structure of myths would lead to the universal properties of the human mind. The structure gives Lévi-Strauss clues about how humanity processes information and narrates stories to compose meaning.

Despite the insights derived from the formal properties of myths Barthes and Lévi-Strauss both incited opposition to their methods. Both offended the traditional scholars who used historical context as the validating criterion for stories and myths. On the one hand Barthes was opposed by Raymond Picard (b. 1917), a Sorbonne professor and specialist on Jean Racine, who accused Barthes of being too arbitrary, impressionistic, and humorless in creating a "new criticism."[4] According to him, Barthes was not respectful enough of the historical and cultural circumstances of myths. Similarly, Lévi-Strauss was castigated by Jean-Paul Sartre (1905-1980), the existentialist philosopher, for not engaging historical detail in the analysis of myths. Marcel Detienne, a practitioner of the functionalist and philological structuralist methods, accused Lévi-Strauss of being too abstract in his analysis of the Oedipus myth (see Chapter Three). Both Barthes and Lévi-Strauss were faulted for not properly using the scientific methods of the linguists by Georges Mounin (b. 1910), a leading linguist and semiologist.

This opposition to the formalist agenda led to the creation of an alternative version of structuralism by Jean-Pierre Vernant, then a professor of classics at the Ecole Pratique des Hautes Études. Inspired by Louis Gernet (1882-1962), a scholar of Greek law who had considerable theoretical influence on Vernant and his colleagues at the Ecole Pratique, Vernant advocated learning as much detail as possible about a culture and its historical and geographical setting before analyzing a myth structurally. With this agenda he organized in 1975 what is now the Louis Gernet Center for the Comparative Study of Ancient Societies to conduct structural analysis within a philological context. Marcel Detienne soon joined him there. In addition, Pierre Vidal-Naquet, a historian with a background in journalism and investigative reporting, and Nicole Loraux, a philologist with interests in the psychology of women in classical Greece, have provided the core for the contextualist school of French structuralist myth analysis.

Before continuing with detailed presentations of each contributor, let us consider what is meant by the concept "structure" and why is it that the French have invested so much in this kind of myth analysis.

STRUCTURE AS A BUILDING BLOCK

The word "structure" comes from *struere* in Latin meaning "building." The term refers to the framework or scaffolding of a building. In the linguistic circles of Europe during the 1920s and '30s this "structure" was used to describe the sound (phonetic) components of language. Nikolai

Troubetskoy (1890-1938), the founder of phonology and a member of the Prague School of linguistics, claimed that historical explanations are inadequate to explain the phonetic similarities in different languages. In 1933 he proposed a model for classifying the distinctive features that separated units of meaning (phonemes) in sounds. This model entails a binary method, with a "+" or a "-" sign at the head of columns, to indicate the presence or absence of a phonemic feature such as voicing or non-voicing--e.g., the difference in sound and meaning between a "z" and an "s" in English.

Troubetskoy's work was spread in the United States during the 1940s by Roman Jakobson, who emigrated to New York's New School for Social Research. There Lévi-Strauss met Jakobson and learned about Troubetskoy's binary taxonomic categories. Lévi-Strauss and Jakobson would later collaborate on an article analyzing a French poem by Charles Baudelaire titled "Les Chats" ("The Cats").[5]

Meanwhile Lévi-Strauss adopted the terms of structural linguistics for anthropology. He had been studying anthropology in Brazil during the early 1930s and had collected oral myths from the Indian tribes of South America. In New York he began to apply the binary methods of Troubetskoy to resolve contradictions in the narratives of these myths. His method proceeds by constructing polar tensions of meaning—tensions similar to the distinctive features plotted by Troubetskoy.

For example, in Lévi-Strauss' reading of the Oedipus myth the category of autochthony, meaning "born of the earth" rather than of woman, leads to understanding why certain characters have privileged behavior. Cadmus, an ancestor of Oedipus, is reputed to have been born of the earth. This origin stands opposed to normal blood relations, which are attributed to births from women. Lévi-Strauss identifies four poles according to whether characters possess autochthonous or normal relations with others. With a grid based on these distinctions, he then resolves the contradictions of patricide and incest in Oedipus, the beloved king and savior of a people from the Sphinx. This schema of the Oedipus myth (see Chapter Three) is characteristic of Lévi-Strauss' tendency to reproduce visually a myth or group of myths on a grid with intersecting axes representing bundles of derived mythical information. Typically, the resulting grid or graph displays the principles around which Lévi-Strauss explains the structures of myths. These principles integrate the content and form of myths. His is not a search for the origin of myth. Instead, he seeks to demonstrate that myth is above all "a logical instrument"[6] transcending the apparent contradictions observed by "civilized" listeners or readers who impose monocultural standards on myths from other cultures. The resourceful ingenuity of the anthropologist or the reader is also called upon to look beyond appearances and retrieve a hidden logical structure.

The survivalist group of French structuralists, inspired by Lévi-Strauss and Barthes, is intent upon revealing the cultural appeal of unrecognized codes in myths. These codes are called "homologies" or language structures expressing similarities. The similarities produced through these homologies exemplify the lesson of myth analysis for Barthes: that myth does not hide anything.[7] After a careful discovery of the misleading contradictions of the appearances of myths, the reasons that a myth is still appealing reveal themselves. Both Barthes and Lévi-Strauss use complex arguments to show these transparent meanings of myth. To many of their readers this transparency of myth is not so obvious. Likewise scholars of written myths do not agree at all with Barthes and Lévi-Strauss about the transparency of myths. When Lévi-Strauss turns to the written myth of Oedipus and applies logical schematics to the Cadmus legend of autochthonous humanity, Vernant and Detienne are disappointed with the absence of references to known historical scholarship about the setting for this well-known myth.

The creation of abstract models from myths is problematic. Lévi-Strauss works with myth in the manner of Joseph Campbell, as reported by Robert Segal: "Just as Campbell severs myths from their narrative context, so he severs them from their social one."[8] Myth is being cut away from the whole to which it belonged originally and to which

it provided an animating life. However, the method of
structural analysis still has much to offer the study of myths.
Vernant and Detienne prefer to say that they are using the
structural method to enhance their work but that they do not
adhere to a whole structuralist ideology by which the structure
explains all meaning in a myth or any other narrative text. The
formal model of the structuralist analysis of myths is
instructive in showing how the human mind works. When,
however, a myth is inscribed within a particular culture, the
myth becomes what the Marxist theorist Fredric Jameson calls
"a whole social and collective mirror image."[9] In order to
retain this social consciousness of myth, the contextualist
school of Vernant and Detienne studies the narrator, the
listener, and the story of a myth within the cultural setting.

According to this school, the variation of Oedipus
invented by Lévi-Strauss the *bricoleur* vitiates the cultural
setting in which Sophocles (496-06 B.C.), for example,
transmitted Oedipus through his tragic trilogy. The politics of
the city-state, the conflict of *logos/muthos*, and the complex
ties of myth and tragedy cannot be ignored. Within the
classical Greek setting myth is an explanation of humanity's
relationships with other humans, the gods, and animals. The
problems of timelessness for the gods and of gender for
humanity are key issues in the Greek myths. Lévi-Strauss
avoids both issues by identifying Oedipus in an autochthonous
framework in which women and time are not part of the
human dilemma for Oedipus. Detienne responds by stipulating
that Greek myth participates in the three orders of the city-
state: the divine, the human, and the animal. The political
body was so important that the Greeks of the fourth century
B.C. even added the goddess of persuasion, Peitho, to the
pantheon.[10] Civic discussion surrounded the evolution of the
Greek city as myths waned in popularity. Peitho joined other
mythical women responsible for the human predicament.
Pandora the first woman instigated the separation of men from
gods and the accompanying scourge of death to humanity.
Hestia, goddess of the hearth, inspired no narrative yet traced
the locus of the housewife in the promised Land of Happily
Ever After.[11] Athena, the virgin, the nonmother, and the

goddess of wisdom, incarnated the contradiction of women's situation as ever-present noncitizens of ancient Greek society. In this environment Oedipus and his pursuit of self-knowledge becomes a tragic myth staged for the discussion of the nature of human virtue. Vernant and his colleagues insist that written myths like that of Oedipus cannot be analyzed in the same way as oral myths. And so a breach appeared within French structuralism to restore myths to their social and ideological milieu.

THE FRENCH HERITAGE

First of all, why is there a French variant of structuralism? Many of the scholars of structuralism are natives of other cultures. However, they all published their works in French in Paris-based publishing houses. Their publication in French gives them the right to be identified as French, as opposed to the Prague, Copenhagen, or Yale schools of structuralism. The tenets of the French writers are also based on French traditions in sciences beginning with René Descartes (1596-1650), who, by the application of mathematical logic, provided the model for reason as the sole basis for deducing scientific truth. The scientific spirit continued in Auguste Comte (1798-1857). Comte founded positivism, the empirical philosophy exemplifying truth as derived from sense experience. Émile Durkheim (1858-1917) began applying the empirical spirit in the social sciences with the invention of sociology. He inspired both Lucien Lévy-Bruhl (1857-1939), who advocated the study of prelogical and mystical thinking, and Marcel Mauss (1873-1950), whose study of gifts (*Essai sur le don*, 1934) was very influential as a model for positing a framework for social relationships. Cultural anthropology, called ethnology in France, grew out of the mixture of these various exponents of scientific truth. It is in this line that Claude Lévi-Strauss assumed his identity as an ethnologist in 1934 when he went to Brazil for three years.

Lévi-Strauss achieved both fame and notoriety with the publication of his *Tristes Tropiques* in 1955. This was his travel log as an ethnologist among Amazon Indian tribes during the 1930s. It was there that he was introduced to the world of myth. From 1958 to 1968 he was the leading voice of French structuralism and published many books propounding the "structuralist" analysis of myth as an alternative to the historical approach. For him, a historical approach is evolutionary: myth is seen by moderns as a product of inferior primitives, their cultural forerunners. Lévi-Strauss theorizes that the human mind is the same everywhere, so that he denies the superiority of "civilized" to "primitive" peoples. The "civilized" setting of the late 1950s included the Cold War, the threat of atomic warfare, and the French colonial struggles in Vietnam and in Algeria. The myths of peoples isolated from this so-called civilization became popular, as did the methods of the new discipline of structural linguistics, which also was an alternative to a historical orientation, and that of philology, which is the study of the sources of words, their etymons. Lévi-Strauss applies the model of structural linguistics analogically to myths as language systems and thus argues that the human mind has a similar structure no matter where or when the expression occurs.

In Paris, where fashion reigns in intellectual endeavors as much as in other ones, there is considerable jockeying for leadership among the various groups. Within French structuralism, the survivalists, the functionalists, and the philologists have vied for leadership. Lévi-Strauss developed his survivalist theories about the nature of structuralism during the late 1950s and then, during the early 1960s, found himself enmeshed in debates about the tenets of structuralism with Sartre, Vernant, the hermeneutical philosopher Paul Ricoeur (b. 1913), and the British anthropologist Edmund Leach (1910-1990). Then Vernant presented his alternative of a contextualist method at the 1967 conference on structuralism at Johns Hopkins University.[12] There the yet unknown philosopher Jacques Derrida (b. 1930) challenged Vernant for being too realistic. Nevertheless, Vernant's "realism" has had a welcome reception from classicists because of his refusal to bend philology for the sake of higher philosophical stakes. At the same time there are considerable differences in method

and result among Vernant, Marcel Detienne, Pierre Vidal-
Naquet, Nicole Loraux, and the succeeding generation of
scholars they have inspired. Each of these variations warrants
a separate introduction.

Vernant was organizing a group to promote his own
structural approach to the study of Greek myths in particular
while Lévi-Strauss was constantly defending his method. The
ethnologist thus attracted attention to the study of myths while
also incurring rancor for the way he analyzed them. Sartre, the
existentialist philosopher who advocated the maximum
involvement of humanity with the social problems of a
historical moment, charged Lévi-Strauss with being
historically inauthentic because the "structuralist" orientation
precluded the historical elements of Sartre's preferred
dialectical method. For Sartre, the dialectic is a term derived
from Karl Marx (1818-1883). According to Marx, the classes
of society are in constant struggle to achieve their goals and
identity. The dialectical method entails the commitment of the
individual to that struggle of the classes. For Sartre, Lévi-
Strauss is not "dialectically engaged" with the tribes who
narrated the myths. In fact, Lévi-Strauss made very few field
trips to collect the myths for his four-volume *Mythologiques*.
Generally, he analyzes the myths with the Cartesian method of
applied mathematical rigor. Instead of the dialectical method
of being personally involved in the collection of data and
entailing the social history of the tribes in the presentation of
their myths, Lévi-Strauss brings together myths of different
peoples, places, and moments as examples of the collective
"human spirit." He is opposed to the monocultural approach
generally implied by the primary investigator's presentations
of the cultures of others. By presenting the common logic or
logics of myths collected from various times and places, Lévi-
Strauss offers a view of human thinking that transcends the
limitations of monocultural reductions of myth to
interpretations by dominant cultures.

Of course, to transcend is to rise above. Lévi-Strauss sees
myth as part of an abstract intellectual paradigm. Paul Ricoeur
criticizes Lévi-Strauss for ignoring the context within which
myths operate—that of mythology. Since myth is a form of

narration existing in time with a beginning and an ending, myth belongs to a social web of rites and symbols. Rather than Lévi-Strauss' insistence that myths lead us directly to the structures of human thinking, Ricoeur encourages Lévi-Strauss to consider the subordination of myth to symbol because "there is no myth without a hint of mythology."[13] Both Ricoeur and Sartre object to Lévi-Strauss' indifference to the larger contexts of myths.

In response, Lévi-Strauss provides a rare case for the "ethnographic context": his analysis of the Asdiwal myth from the Pacific coast of Canada.[14] This context is the setting that a writer of ethnological narratives must prepare before beginning to write. By explaining the geographic, economic, sociological, and cosmological settings for this myth, Lévi-Strauss invents a model for explaining myth on what he calls horizontal and vertical axes. These axes are derived from Jakobson, who invented a grid of the horizontal axis for metaphor (the literal identification of two unlike items—e.g., "The eagle spoke as a chieftain") and the vertical axis for metonymy (the substitution of one thing for another without explicit linkages—e.g., "The Kremlin [rather than the Soviet President] rejected the American plea for peace") to explain a text linguistically. Whereas the literary use of metonymy entails the literal substitution of one thing for another, Jakobson describes the operation of this substitution on the same literal plane, which he calls the horizontal axis. The use of metaphor is by analogy and requires an imaginative leap outside the literal realm. Jakobson plots metaphor on what he calls the vertical axis. The grid of these two axes conveniently diagrams the use of language and is found throughout Lévi-Strauss' own writings as a means to plot the intersection of the languages of the many myths he collects. With such a grid Lévi-Strauss constructs a matrix within which myth and the various factors attributable to its historical context can be analyzed with horizontal and vertical axes.

Despite his concession to his critics who object to his usually dismissive attitude toward historical factors, Lévi-Strauss remained committed in his promotion of the formal presence of the "human spirit," the universal presence of the same patterns in human thinking. Ricoeur accused him of being Kantian in his insistence on the categorical imperative, or the innate determination, of the human spirit. Lévi-Strauss took the appellation Kantian as a compliment and did not return to the Asdiwal example of the "contextualist method" in other analytical exercises.

Excepting Lévi-Strauss' Asdiwal analysis, Jean-Pierre Vernant objects to Lévi-Strauss in his lack of sensitivity to the general interaction of a written myth with its historical setting. Since much more is known about the history and geographical setting of written myths than is known about the myths of oral traditions, the setting often provides pertinent clues about the relationship of the myth to its originating culture. The survivalist attitude about myths concentrates more on the similarities of one myth to other myths. Since the survivalists, Barthes and Lévi-Strauss, focus on oral traditions, they assume that myths have an internal cohesion and logic that can be analyzed without explaining the interaction of myths with their readers.

Nevertheless, the structuralist orientation appeals to Vernant. It helps him make new connections between myth and society. Building on Lévi-Strauss' ethnographic model of Asdiwal he introduces the influences of words and change upon the Greek myths. Vernant is more sensitive than Lévi-Strauss to the influences of cultural change upon myth. He often uses the historical study of Greek words done by philologists to analyze the changes in philosophical concepts over time and their influence on concepts in myths. Such words as "justice," "family," "slave," and "household" are insightful for their concomitant evolution with the development of Greek self-governance in the city-states during the fourth and fifth centuries B.C.

In order to attract scholars who could help to identify the changing concepts which affected the contexts of Greek myths, Vernant founded the Gernet Center in 1975 as a research base fostering this variant of structuralism. There he insists that myths be described in their internal and external cohesion and that their geographical and historical contexts be applied to an analysis of the mythological network in which a single myth exists. Vernant thus applies a spatial and temporal grid within which myths are to be appreciated.

For example, Vernant's presentation, with Marcel Detienne, of "cunning intelligence" (*mètis*) is especially representative of a new "liberal philology,"[15] in which the myths of Greek antiquity are placed in relationships exemplifying balance. Hermes, for example, is a cunning god who is the master of snares and the inspiration for hunters and fishermen. His model of resourcefulness for men must be seen as the counterbalance to Hestia, the goddess of the hearth and the model for women as guardians of family values within the evolving Greek city state. The Greek concepts of household, justice, and family influenced the central place that these two gods played in the daily lives of the Greeks.

During the 1970s Vernant attracted noteworthy scholars to his contextualist cause in Paris. Marcel Detienne and Pierre Vidal-Naquet joined him at the Ecole Pratique, and Vidal-Naquet succeeded Vernant as Director of the Center. All three have collaborated to provide a unique kind of structural method emanating from the Center. Some works are joint projects of the Center.[16] Each participant, however, has a separate and clearly defined interest and agenda.

Detienne is the figure most involved in distinguishing the method of the contextualists from the formalism of Lévi-Strauss. Himself a former Lévi-Straussian, Detienne is a philologist in orientation as opposed Vernant, whose basic orientation is that of a philosopher and psychologist. Detienne advocates more respect for philology, for the role of words and their evolution in myths, and for change in written myths. Written myths are anchors in the evolution of the cultures to which they belong. Stylistically, Detienne effectively uses Socratic questions to whet the appetites of his readers as he examines the underlying assumptions of classical myths. His questions are never directly answered and are reminiscent of Paul Gauguin's exploration of myth by titling his paintings as questions.

Pierre Vidal-Naquet complements Detienne by addressing the political and ideological motives for myths. Vidal-Naquet brings to the Center an anti-racist penchant from his opposition to the Algerian War. He signed the Manifesto of the 121 against the War and wrote a pamphlet revealing the French Army's tactics of torture during the War. He also analyzed various revisionist myths denying the Holocaust. Preferring not to be labeled a structuralist but rather an advocate of structural analysis, Vidal-Naquet presents this analysis as a heuristic instrument for the exploration of classical myth. As a historian, he views myth as the repository for the collective memory of a social group. In addition to the revisionist myths about the Holocaust, he has written about the political myths of the Golden Age of Greece, Plato's myth of the statesman, and the May '68 revolts in France.

Nicole Loraux completes the first generation of Gernet Center scholars as a student and now as a colleague to Vernant and Vidal-Naquet. Her interests in sociology, philology, psychology, and the roles of women in Greek society have been especially valuable in developing the interests in women's issues initially suggested by Vernant, Detienne, and Vidal-Naquet. Loraux has made valuable contributions with her analysis of funeral speeches in Athens and the ways in which women are allowed to die in Greek myths and tragedies. She explores the rhetorical models for women in the city-state. While death became the occasion for perpetuating the immortality of the city-state in funeral orations, the deaths of women had no glory at all and instead became the occasion for observing silence. Loraux explores the myths of Athena and Pandora as role models for women in a society in which the presence of women was a reminder of men's separation from the company of the gods. Loraux views myth as knowledge serving rhetorically as an argument for the ideological positioning of one social group vis-à-vis another. This rhetorical role of myth—myth as the conveyor of argument and social experiment—leads Loraux to examine the relationships of discourse to the gender roles of Greek society. Her insights into the discourses of Greek men and women are especially inspirational for a second generation of scholars who are making their mark especially in the semiotic and artistic dimensions of Greek myths.

This younger generation of contextualists also brings enthusiasm for the development of the stakes established by Vernant, Detienne, and Vidal-Naquet. There is the emerging importance of François Hartog, Suzanne Saïd, and Florence Dupont. Hartog, who is being translated into English as part of the program for "new historicism" in the United States, rereads Herodotus (c.484-25 B.C.), the father of history, in such a way that his telling is appreciated as reflective of the discourse of his era. Saïd, who is on the university faculty at Strasbourg, is reexamining the contextualist stakes in the myths of Prometheus. Dupont, whose research is supported by the Gernet Center, exposes the banquet as a paradigm for the relationships between pleasure and the law from Plato to the *Satyricon* (1 A.D.). In *Le Plaisir et la loi* (1977) she develops the arguments for a prereferential language in the *logos sympotikos*,[17] which is based on a tradition extending from Plato's *Symposium*.

I will examine each of these contributors to the French structural approach to myth. Let us look first at Roland Barthes, whose formalist methods brought international popularity to the analysis of myths.

NOTES

1. Claude Lévi-Strauss, *La Pensée sauvage* (Paris: Plon, 1962) (tr. *The Savage Mind* [Chicago: University of Chicago Press, 1966]). See especially the chapter "La Science du concret" ("The Science of the Concrete") for his presentation of *bricolage*.

2. See my *French Structuralism* (Boston: Twayne World Author Series, 1990), chap. 1, for a discussion of the competing claims and parameters of the various "structuralist" schools of thought.

3. Roland Barthes, *Mythologies*, tr. Annette Lavers (New York: Hill & Wang, 1972), p. 109.

4. Raymond Picard, *Nouvelle critique ou nouvelle imposture?* (Utrecht: Pauvert, 1965). Picard is especially concerned in this pamphlet with how Barthes has created a mythology of his "new criticism" and has encouraged, in his *Sur Racine* (1963), a misleading reading of Jean Racine's theater.

5.Roman Jakobson and Claude Lévi-Strauss, "'Les Chats' de Charles Baudelaire," *L'Homme*, II (January-April 1962), pp. 5-21.

6. Claude Lévi-Strauss, *Anthropologie structurale* (Paris: Plon, 1958), pp. 239-43.

7. Roland Barthes, *Mythologies* (Paris: Editions du Seuil, 1957), p. 207. Also Lavers tr. p. 121.

8. Robert A. Segal, *Joseph Campbell: An Introduction* (New York: Garland, 1987), p. 138.

9. Fredric Jameson, *The Ideologies of Theory*, vol. 2 (Minneapolis: University of Minnesota Press, 1988), p. 151.

10. See I. F. Stone, *The Trial of Socrates* (Boston: Little, Brown, 1988), pp. 205ff. Athena required the Furies to "recognize the majesty of Peitho" as the new goddess of persuasion since open discussion became crucial in the democratic government of Athens.

11. See Kathryn Allen Rabuzzi, *The Sacred and the Feminine: Toward a Theology of Housework* (New York: Seabury Press, 1982), on the effects of the absence of myths about Hestia the goddess of the hearth in the mythology of housewifery.

12. A collection of the lectures and discussions appeared as *The Structuralist Controversy: The Languages of Criticism and the Sciences of Man*, ed. Richard Macksey and Eugenio Donato (Baltimore: Johns Hopkins University Press, 1970).

13. Paul Ricoeur, *The Conflict of Interpretations*, tr. Don Ihde (Evanston: Northwestern University Press, 1974), p. 29.

14. Claude Lévi-Strauss, "La Geste d'Asdiwal," in *Anthropologie structurale II* (Paris: Plon, 1973), tr. N. Mann as "The Story of Asdiwal" in *Structural Anthropology II* (Chicago: University of Chicago Press, 1976), pp. 146-97.

15. This term was invented by Robert Pogue Harrison in his review of the collaborative work by Vernant and Detienne in "The Ambiguities of Philology," *Diacritics*, XVI, 2 (Summer 1986), 14ff.

16. For example, the collaborative activities as members of the Gernet Center have produced the already mentioned *Les Ruses de l'intelligence* (Paris: Flammarion, 1974), tr. *Cunning Intelligence in Greek Culture and Society* (1978), by Detienne and Vernant; *La Cuisine du sacrifice en pays grec* (Paris: Gallimard, 1979), tr. *The Cuisine of Sacrifice Among the Greeks* (1989), by Detienne and Vernant; *Mythe et tragédie en Grèce Ancienne* (Paris: Maspero, 1972; vol. 2, Paris: La Découverte, 1986), tr. *Myth and Tragedy in Ancient Greece* (1988), by Vernant and Vidal-Naquet.

17. Florence Dupont, *Le Plaisir et la loi* (Paris: Maspero, 1977), pp. 39ff.

Chapter Two

BARTHES: MYTH AS MEANINGFUL FORM

From 1954 to 1956 Roland Barthes wrote a regular column for the newspaper *Les Lettres nouvelles* entitled "The Mythology of the Month." This column discussed the hidden meanings of aspects and items of life in France. The mythologies were his meanings for unsuspected myths in the day-to-day experiences of the French. The myths were the stories that connected the objects to French culture. Barthes' subjects ranged from popular song as bourgeois art to the Tour de France as epic to wine as a national totem. Prior to Barthes' proclamations of the myths of France, the French neither gave these objects any manifest meaning nor identified them as myths. His approach was structuralist because he discovered latent connections between these objects and assumptions about the nature of French culture as an identifiable narrative to which these myths contributed elaborating chapters.

In 1953 Barthes wrote in the same newspaper that the analysis of myths was "the only effective manner for an intellectual to be involved politically."[1] This political involvement entailed the exposition of ideologies implied by the hidden structures of meaning in myths. Barthes was being dialectically involved in the struggle of society's existence, thus fulfilling Jean-Paul Sartre's call for the intellectual's responsibility in society.

During the early 1950s, mythology was for Barthes "a delusion to be explored," as literary critic Jonathan Culler has expressed it.[2] The "delusion" was Barthes' belief in the methods of semiology, the linguistic study of signs according

21

to Ferdinand de Saussure (1857-1913), one of the theoreticians
of structural linguistics. The model of semiology inspired
Barthes to claim that an item possessed a hidden structure
along with a mythical story. For example, wrestling was
popular entertainment in France during the early 1950s.
Barthes presents this spectacle as the manifestation of a
symbolic contest for Good and Evil, a specifically French
ethical struggle that transcends political associations with the
acting out of Suffering, Humiliation, and the ultimate
resolution of Justice. The political references are to wrestling
in the United States at a time when wrestlers were identified
with politically tainted ideologies (e.g., the title "Red" for a
Communist). For Barthes, French wrestlers are like priests in
a religious ceremony. The spectators are transported by the
experience. The change is brought about by the cathartic
effect of participating in the suffering and humiliation of the
wrestlers within the context of Good and Evil struggling to
bring about Justice. Inevitably, the spectators leave with a
sense of justice in that the Good wrestler prevails, thus
validating Justice naively thought to be working in their daily
lives.

   Although this analysis might have been achieved by
many a nonstructuralist, Barthes claims a structuralist identity
for his approach. The approach is "structuralist" in that it
identifies a cohesive, hidden identity. Barthes focuses on the
survival of some cultural items and attributes this survival to
their mythical "forms." Forms are those organic features of
cultural items which allow them to survive the test of time.
Barthes views such forms as mythologized when they assume
narrative coherence for a culture. Of course, the narrative is
elaborated by Barthes rather than by the culture. He is a seer
who makes manifest what is implied in the usage of the object
in the daily lives of the bourgeois. The constructed narrative
gives the reasons for the survival of the myth by explaining
the relationship of the myth to the values of society, as in the
example of wrestling as a religious enactment of justice.
Barthes' narration provides the verbal component for the story
and its latent ties between an artifact and its culture. This
reconstruction of myths by Barthes is in sharp contrast to

myths found in cultures such as ancient Greece, where the stories are already narrated and where only the connection to the culture must be established. Nevertheless, Barthes contributes the art of connecting the myth to a culture through his development of the implied scaffolding that links what has survived with the values of a culture.

MYTH AS A KIND OF SPEECH

What Roland Barthes called "mythologies" were also collected in an anthology with that name in 1957. An extensive essay, "Myth Today," which is appended to that collection, offers insights into the nature of structuralist analysis as a tool for explaining the survival of myths. This anthology appeared about a year after the publication of Claude Lévi-Strauss' very popular *Tristes Tropiques*. Not only did Lévi-Strauss' popularity enhance the Barthes work, but some of their common critics claim that Barthes' method was a loosely applied adaptation of the misguided linguistics of Lévi-Strauss.[3] Despite these barbs, to which I will return at the end of this chapter, there is much to be learned from "Myth Today" about the structuralist stance on myths.

Like Lévi-Strauss, Barthes is concerned with explaining the survival of myths. While Lévi-Strauss presents myth as an elaboration of the "human spirit," Barthes grounds myth in its language. Like speech, myth is motivated by that which surrounds it. This "motivation" determines a myth's meaning and provides a linguistic setting for meaning similar to the context advocated by the Gernet Center scholars. Barthes says that there is no myth without a "motivated form."[4] In effect, this motivation is Barthes' nod to the historical effect on mythical form. Accordingly, the myth of wrestling for the French in the early 1950s provides a basis for the survival of clearly defined moral codes after the confusing messages of the Occupation, collaboration, and the purge trials. The activity of wrestling was mythologized by French culture because its mythology provided an ethical narrative explaining the survival of Good and Evil by which the French might

judge other contemporary features such as the Cold War,
colonial campaigns, and the threat of atomic war. Barthes
therefore attributes the survival of myth to its serving a
contemporary social need. The "motivated form" of a myth is typically hidden from
view. Social need and language combine to provide   the
motivation for the survival of a myth. For example, Barthes
invokes the psychoanalytic analysis of myth as a paradigm for
the disguised motivated form. Sigmund Freud (1856-1939)
recalls the Oedipus myth from Sophocles' *Oedipus the King* (c.
431 B.C.). The paradigm of the family triangle as the basis for
the socialization of human sexuality represents the social need
for Freud. The sexual desires of a son for his mother, at the
expense of his father, constitute Freud's explanation of the
self's search for the social other. Barthes notes that language
provides a disguise for the newly motivated myth, in this case
the Sophoclean story, with a neologism, in this case, the
"Oedipus complex." Thus social need and language contribute
to the motivated form of myth.

Barthes' structuralist perspective of myth does not end
with his focusing on the motivation of a myth. He explains his
method as analyzing "the body of intentions which have
motivated it [myth] and arranged it there as the signal of an
individual history."[5] This "individual history" found in the
motivation of myths distinguishes Barthes from Lévi-Strauss
who has a general disregard for history. In some of the debates
about structuralism such as the one with Raymond Picard of
the Sorbonne during the mid-1960s, Barthes was accused of
vitiating history because of his association with the
structuralism of Lévi-Strauss.[6] However, as we shall see,
Barthes has a unique view of history as it applies within the
structuralist framework of myth analysis.

AN INDIVIDUAL HISTORY

For Barthes, events of the day cause an individual sign to be mythologized and transformed into something greater than itself. For example, the medical community at the end of the nineteenth century was so sure of itself and intent upon healing maladies called neuroses that some members of the community restructured their careers to become psychoanalysts, thus investing great power in the myth of the Oedipus complex as narrated by Freud. Barthes would probably call the Oedipus complex a second-order myth. This is a myth based on another myth and transforms the first one to such an extent that it calls into question the very viability of the original myth. The Oedipus myth is better known in the psychoanalytic version than in the version narrated by Sophocles.

Barthes portrays myth as a part of ideology, the non-conscious thinking by a culture of itself. As an ideological construction, myth uses symbols, words that mean something other than their literal meaning, to portray a culture's values. Wrestling, as we have seen, is such an example for the France of the 1950s. Such mythical symbols require a certain kind of interpretation. Barthes calls himself a semiologist in this role as interpreter of mythical symbols. A semiologist explains the functioning of signs according to the model of language. Barthes' description of myth as a speech act is crucial to understanding his presentation of myth as a form of language. The structure of a myth is tripartite, as is a sign. Like (1) a sign linking (2) a concept to (3) a meaning, (1) a myth uses multiple signs within its (2) form to invent (3) signification. Myth is thus a second-order sign. The structure of a myth is similar to that of a sign in that its meaning is distinct from its conceptualization and its representation. The survival of the myth in its representation is largely the result of a culture's ideological weaving of the myth into the fabric of a culture. This weaving is done by the use of symbols so that the literal sense of a myth is given additional meaning by the ideology of a culture.

For Barthes, the symbolic values attributed to myths occur within an ideology. The symbolic and thus ideological meanings given to myths constitute what Barthes calls the myth's "alibi." This linking gives value to the individual history of a myth. The literal story of a myth is not ideological. The meaning of the myth accounts for a culture's ideology and thus provides the alibi of a myth. The alibi is so effective in rallying the beliefs of a social group about a myth that, for Barthes, myth does away with the need for dialectical explanations, necessitated by his commitment to Marxist history. The issue of the dialectical struggle led Jean-Paul Sartre to dispute with Lévi-Strauss about the disengagement of structuralist myth analysis. In other words, in the structuralist models offered by Lévi-Strauss, there is no concern for a myth's acceptance within a cultural context. By contrast, Barthes explains that the alibi of a myth indicates the ties between myth and culture as the struggle for the survival of a given myth. The alibi grounds the myth in the unconscious values promoted by a culture. This role of the alibi allows for the compatibility of structuralism with history. Barthes says that a little structuralism turns one away from history, but that a lot brings one back to history. It is a question of a measured approach, which the Gernet Center scholars—especially Vidal-Naquet—took seriously in their own agenda. The question to ask now is what kind of history is compatible with the structure of myth.

In exploring the relationship between history and structure, Barthes calls the distortion of the structure by the alibi a game of hide-and-seek. The literal story of the myth is hidden by its acknowledged meaning for a given group. This hiding activity of myth is the social manifestation of the myth disguising the myth's original identity with social motivation. Barthes calls this "language robbery"[7] because speech is stolen from its original context and reinserted in a new semantic order. He does not portray the signification or new meaning of myth as an unconscious one. In fact, he insists that there is no play of the unconscious in the second-order meaning. For Barthes, myth is a game of surfaces covering one another. The semiologist must uncover these surfaces to reveal what the meaning, or signification, of a myth is for a culture.

Since myth is a surface text without hierarchical structuring, Barthes portrays the signification of a myth as a spatial problem with no recourse to symbolic systems. A symbolic system is an abstract network of meanings in addition to the original literal meaning of a sign. Mythical structure does not take over a sign system by merely making it more abstract and giving it an additional meaning. Instead, mythical structure makes a substitution for the original meaning by shifting the speech act to another place within another neighborhood. The vocabulary used is clearly not temporal or historical but rather spatial or geographical. Rather than the abstract meanings of symbolic activity, myth entails the passing of the meaning in a sign system to a concrete form in which the setting of a concept imbeds a different meaning. This meaning of myth is never in the same place as is the form of myth. In other words, meaning, similar to the alibi of myth, does not occupy the same space as the form of myth. The semiologist looks elsewhere for mythical form, alibi, and meaning.

MYTH AS A GLOBAL SIGN

Myth assumes the properties of a global sign--a sign that creates its own world and subsumes other systems in its course. A global sign can also be recognized by other cultures as having value and meaning as a human form of communication. Because of the wide scope of a global sign myth can be read in multiple ways. Barthes identifies three kinds of reading applicable to myth: the cynical, the "demystifying," and the dynamic.

The cynical reading is a literal understanding of the myth as a simple sign. This reading assumes that myth is a form of language conveying a meaning intended by a narrator for a listener. This reading assumes that human communication is no more complex than everyday speech acts, which transfer messages directly to the reader of the myths

without any noise or mediation. For example, the myth of
Oedipus can be read as the story of a man condemned to
unrecognized patricide and incest by the sins of his father:
Laius' infidelity to Jocasta and his introduction of sodomy into
Greece.

The demystifying reading of myth acknowledges that
myths are sign systems in which some distortion of
information takes place. The reader must therefore distinguish
overlapping signs producing noise—i.e., no new
information—from dense signs, which are capable of
producing meaning. But there is bad faith in this kind of
reading because of the assumption that the origins of the
message can be reproduced. Inspired by Descartes' motto
larvatus prodeo ("I advance wearing a mask"), Barthes speaks
of reading the tragedy of Oedipus all the while knowing that
Oedipus will be unmasked.[8] In other words, the reader may
project upon the reading the problems of the self so that
unmasking Oedipus is a solution about the other's role in the
formation of the self. With that solution in mind the reader
chooses which signs will be either helpful or obstructive in
realizing the teleological goal.

The dynamic reading allows for the full polyvalence of
the signification of myths. In order to read myths dynamically,
Barthes promotes the use of the science of semiology to
distinguish the speech act of myth as a separate sign system.
Portraying the heroes of Jean Racine's tragedies in *Sur Racine*,
Barthes notes the duality in their characters as the tragic alibis
of the mythological figures take them in different directions
from their classical sources. For the Oedipus myth the
ambiguity of Oedipus' being driven by fate and by the desire
to know himself reveals a natural human ambivalence. In the
myth, this duality is transmitted by the sequence of the
Theban myths predicting his fate and the tragic flaw necessary
for the credibility of Sophocles' tragic hero.

Barthes' semiological prospectus for myth was short-
lived. In 1971 he renounced his semiological project by saying
that the science of reading had changed and that his project of
distinguishing the ideological from the mythological had itself
become mythical.[9] In fact, the criticism levelled at him by the

linguist and semiologist Georges Mounin[10] was devastating because it accused Barthes of not knowing what the linguistic bases were for his semiology of myth. Barthes says that Lévi-Strauss intervened by encouraging him to stay with written texts but to abandon his project for a semiology under the larger rubric of linguistics.[11] However, Barthes did not continue his work on semiology and myths during the last decade of his lifetime, 1970-80. Some say that his interest in myths and semiology was linked with his pursuit of scientific method.[12] And that method reached its zenith and ironic self-fulfillment with the publication of *S/Z* (1970). He exhausted the scientific method in this reading and therefore turned away from myth analysis.

Barthes laid some important groundwork during his experiments with myths and mythologies. He participated in the structuralist agenda for fifteen years and contributed toward the clarification of a French structuralist method. His portrayal of myth as a speech act set the stage for the adaptation of structural linguistics to myth by Lévi-Strauss. Although Barthes might not have been properly schooled in the sciences of linguistics and semiology, his popular presentation of a scientific attitude toward myth was an important step in encouraging the scientific analysis of myth as a linguistic document.

Barthes also prepared the way for the studies of myth by other French structuralists. On the one hand he preferred an orientation studying the survival of myth and promoted the study of a dynamic reading. This dynamic reading, as a recognition of the ambivalence at the heart of myth, is a forerunner of Lévi-Strauss' view of the structure of myth as the resolution of contradictions. Barthes restricted his conception of myth to a narrative phenomenon in which hidden meanings suggest a game of hide-and-seek between meaning and form. Lévi-Strauss would take exception to the focus on the form as the structure of myth and broaden the arguments of mythical structure to include content as well. Nevertheless, Barthes served an important role with his notion of the ideological alibi of myth which attributes the meaning of myth to culture. In addition, Barthes, in anticipation of

Lévi-Strauss, approached myth neither hermeneutically nor dialectically. These positions proved especially inflammatory to Paul Ricoeur and Jean-Paul Sartre, as I will discuss in the next chapter. On the other hand the Contextualist position was also announced in Barthes' prospectus. His observation that "human history rules the life and death of mythical language"[13] would be confirmed by the members of the Gernet Center. Barthes, however, is generally not cited by the Gernet scholars despite their general inclination to cite generously. The Barthes-Picard debates of the early 1960s ended with Barthes' elevation to a guru figure for the avant-garde. Barthes did not emerge on the side of the historicists despite his earlier claim that myth could not exist without a motivated form. It must be reasserted that for Barthes myth is not dialectical. This observation undermines his whole project of allowing the form of myths to interact with history. Despite his insinuations that cultural forms do not threaten history, his program for the meaningful form of myth in fact precludes the discovery of new historical information since the ideological alibi orients the reading of myths in a teleological manner. Lévi-Strauss offers a more elaborate presentation of the semantic structure of myths and a longer lasting dedication to the program of the structuralist reading of myths.

NOTES

1. Roland Barthes, "Maîtres et esclaves," *Les Lettres nouvelles*, March 1953, p. 108.

2. Jonathan Culler, *Roland Barthes* (New York: Oxford University Press, 1983), p. 33.

3. See Georges Mounin, *Introduction à la sémiologie* (Paris: Minuit, 1970), on Barthes' (pp. 189-98) and Lévi-Strauss' (pp. 199-214) erroneous adaptations of the linguistics

of Louis Hjelmslev (the "semiology" of Barthes) and of Roman Jakobson (Lévi-Strauss' linguistics).

4. Roland Barthes, "Myth Today," in his *Mythologies*, tr. Annette Lavers (New York: Hill & Wang, 1972), p. 126.

5. *Ibid.*, p. 125.

6. See my *Literary History in the Wake of Roland Barthes* (Birmingham, AL.: Summa Publications, 1984) about Barthes' re-introduction of literary history into reading.

7. Barthes, "Myth Today," p. 131.

8. Roland Barthes, *Le Plaisir du texte* (Paris: Seuil, 1973), pp. 75-76.

9. Roland Barthes, "Change the Object Itself," in his *Image Music Text*, ed. and tr. Stephen Heath (New York: Hill & Wang, 1977), p. 166.

10. Mounin, pp. 189-99.

11. Roland Barthes, "Réponses," *Tel Quel*, No. 47 (Fall 1971), 99.

12. For example, Philippe Roger, *Roland Barthes, Roman* (Paris: Grasset et Fasquelle, 1986), pp. 86ff.

13. Barthes, "Myth Today," p. 110.

Chapter Three

LEVI-STRAUSS AND THE PROBLEMS OF OEDIPUS

For Claude Lévi-Strauss, myth is a logical instrument to think through certain contradictions of human experience.[1] Myth makes connections between its inventors and their mysterious world. The connections are not always obvious because myth builds bridges among apparently disconnected phenomena. Lévi-Strauss contrasts myth to history by pointing out that, while history is an open system of communication because it is always adding new information, myth is a closed system of communication because it is a static form with the same elements combined over and over again.[2] The structures discovered by Lévi-Strauss are maps of these elements. The maps recur in many different myths and provide ways to resolve contradictions presented by myths. The logic of these structures is innate to the closed system of the myths. Consequently, Lévi-Strauss says that myths think themselves. There is a logic inherent in myths. The contradictions of history are resolved within the closed limits of the story of the myth. Lévi-Strauss' analysis of the Oedipus myth illustrates the nature of the closed system of myths. In subsequent chapters we will compare his approach to the myth with that of other French structuralists.

Oedipus is supposed to have lived one thousand years before Sophocles immortalized him in the 5th century B.C. Oedipus is doubtless best known because of Freud's adaptation of the Oedipus character from Sophocles' *Oedipus Rex*. Freud's Oedipus has been so popularized that this is the sole Oedipus that most people know. Gilles Deleuze and Félix Guattari note in *Anti-Oedipus* (1972) that "psychoanalysis

doesn't need to invent Oedipus: the subjects introduce
themselves to their psychiatrists already totally oedipalized."[3]
The Oedipus myth is thus a part of the vocabulary of
contemporary culture in the tradition of tragedy that has
become part of the Western experience of growing to
adulthood. Freud's version of Oedipus is that the character
evinces unconscious desires toward his parents. He is attached
to his mother and is resentful of his father. This complex is
based upon Freud's reading of the tragedies about Oedipus
written by Sophocles.

In Sophocles' version, presented in *Oedipus Rex*, *Oedipus
at Colonus*, and *Antigone*, Laius, King of Thebes through the
line of Cadmus, was in exile from Thebes and was staying in
the house of Pelops in Attica. There Laius refused sex with his
wife Jocasta and initiated a homosexual relationship with the
son of Pelops, Chrysippus. As retribution, Pelops cursed Laius
by promising that if a son was born to Laius, that son would
kill his father. Laius and Jocasta did have a son. To preclude
the realization of Pelops' curse, Laius ran a spike through his
son's foot and abandoned him on Mt. Cithaeron. There a
shepherd found him and gave him to Polybus, the King of
Corinth. Since Polybus and his wife, Merope, were childless,
they adopted the abandoned infant and named him Oedipus
("swollen foot").

As a young man, Oedipus was once called a bastard child,
so he went to Delphi to consult Apollo about his parents. The
oracle revealed that Oedipus would not only kill his father but
also marry his mother. He therefore left Corinth, where he
thought his real parents resided, and headed for Thebes. Along
the road Oedipus killed his real father, Laius, in a "chance"
encounter over the right of way. Oedipus proceeded to deliver
Thebes from the Sphinx, which was starving the Thebans and
which destroyed those who could not solve its riddle. Oedipus
did solve the riddle and thus earned the hand of the widowed
Queen, Jocasta. Oedipus and Jocasta had four children:
Eteocles, Polynices, Antigone, and Ismene.

Upon the discovery of the incest, Jocasta hanged herself
and Oedipus put his eyes out with Jocasta's brooch. Oedipus
went into exile at Colonus, where he was cared for by

Antigone, while his sons fought over the throne and Ismene stayed in Thebes to keep Antigone informed about the family feud. Oedipus disappeared from the earth at Colonus. Eteocles and Polynices were killed. Their uncle, Creon, became King of Thebes and did not allow Antigone to bury the bodies of her brothers. When she nevertheless did do so, she was buried alive.

Although Sophocles provides "the canonical version"[4] of the Oedipus myth, Sophocles is not the only Greek or Roman to pay attention to Oedipus. The classical mythologies narrated by Hesiod, Homer, Apollodorus, Aeschylus, and Seneca, among others, present the Theban saga, of which the Oedipus myth is a part. The saga starts with the founding of the city of Thebes by Cadmus, brother of Europa and son of Agenor, King of Tyre. Agenor sends Cadmus and his two brothers to search for their sister Europa, who disappeared because she was abducted by Zeus. Cadmus is advised by the oracle of Delphi to give up the search and to found the city of Thebes. To get water at Thebes he must kill a dragon. The goddess Athena advises Cadmus to sow the dragon's teeth. From these teeth springs an army of men known as the Spartoi ("the sewn men"). They kill one another until only five remain. They become the ancestors of Theban nobility. The royal family line of Cadmus continues through his marriage to Harmonia, daughter of Arès and Aphrodite, until the son of Labdacos, Laius, refuses sex with his wife, Jocasta. Hera, the protectress of marriage, sends the Sphinx to seize Thebes as retribution for Laius' disassociation from his wife.

There also have been many adaptations of the Oedipus story. Pierre Corneille wrote a tragedy (*Oedipe*) about the myth in 1659. The modern era has seen adaptations of Oedipus by Igor Stravinsky (the opera-oratorio *Oedipus Rex*), Pier Pasolini (the film *Edipo Re*), Hugo von Hofmannstall (*Oidipus und die Sphinx*), André Gide (*Oedipe* and *Thésée*), and Jean Cocteau (*La Machine infernale*). The list of adaptations and analogues to the Oedipus myth goes on and on. Lowell Edmunds has compiled the sources and variations in his *Oedipus: The Ancient Legend and its Later Analogues* (Baltimore: Johns Hopkins University Press, 1985). There have

been many interpretations of the story by nonstructuralists, as
exemplified in the anthology and bibliography provided by
Edmunds and Alan Dundes in their *Oedipus: A Folklore
Casebook* (New York: Garland, 1984). Because of its survival and function in many varied
cultures, the myth of Oedipus has fascinated French
structuralists. For Lévi-Strauss, the royal family of Cadmus is
the determining factor in the myth. Cadmus' sowing in the
earth the teeth of monsters to produce the Spartoi, the
ancestors of the Thebans, provides a basis for claims about the
autochthonous ("born of the earth") beginnings of humanity
and sets up one of the contradictions to be addressed by the
structure of the Oedipus myth as cast by Lévi-Strauss. Since
many ancient cultures believed that man was originally born
of the earth, not of woman, and since Lévi-Strauss explicitly
includes in the Oedipus myth "all its versions,"[5] he
incorporates the Cadmus legend in his presentation of the
Oedipus myth.

Originally published in 1955, "The Structural Study of
Myth" breaks down the Oedipus myth into constituent events.
Similar events are grouped in "bundles," which are then
characterized with simple sentences called "mythemes." The
sentences set up relationships within the myth. These
relationships are the semantic structures discovered by Lévi-
Strauss. For the Oedipus myth, there are four bundles of
meanings: 1) the overrating of blood relations, 2) the
underrating of blood relations, 3) the denial of the
autochthonous origins of man, and 4) the persistence of the
autochthonous origins of man. These categories are the
common features for each column of events presented in the
diagram (translated on p. 41). The specific grid, composed of
horizontal and vertical sequences, is actually two readings
interacting with each other in the same diagram. Lévi-Strauss
organizes this grid to show his respect for the literal or
horizontal sequence of events (what Barthes calls a cynical
reading) juxtaposed with his own structural reading, based on
a paradigmatic organization of these same events in order to
provide a vertical (Barthes' dynamic reading) reading of the
myth that would respect the ambiguity of its contradictions on

the horizontal axis. This ambiguity can then be recast in a positive way to speak about the inherent ambivalence of myths. The four columns chart the greater or lesser degree of either characteristic by organizing sentences that express a relationship—e.g., Oedipus marries his mother Jocasta. This sentence is placed in the column with the common feature of the overrating of blood relations, as exemplified by their incest. The other columns feature the underrating of blood relations, the denial of the autochthonous origin of man, and the persistence of the autochthonous origin of man. All four columns exemplify the inherent denial of the categories of blood relationships. They thereby affirm autochthony. The diagram is thus an example of Lévi-Strauss' logical model of how myth overcomes the apparent contradiction between humans born from one and humans born from two. He concludes that "the inability to connect two kinds of relationships is overcome (or rather replaced) by the positive statement that contradictory relationships are identical inasmuch as they are both self-contradictory in a similar way."[6]

By contast with the network of relationships Lévi-Strauss identifies here, the Oedipus myth is also a rich mine for the philological search for origins that characterizes much of the contextual camp of French myth analysis. The origins of words were part of the fascination of the Greeks themselves with myth. Oedipus, he with the "swollen foot" who is condemned to being crippled and off-balance, is a good source for a discussion of the Greek notion of virtue (*arete*). The balance so absent in Oedipus is absent as well in his grandfather Labdacos ("left-handed," thus out of synchrony with the right-handed majority). While Socrates teaches that virtuous people are those who know, Sophocles portrays Oedipus as stubbornly pursuing self-knowledge and self-destruction in the same desire. The written version of the myth in the tragedies by Sophocles especially interests Vernant and his colleagues because of the specificity of its details. Vernant and Marcel Detienne learned from Louis Gernet about the Greek legal system, which placed virtue and

knowledge within the context of other values for the Greeks.
For example, Zeus had also given to humanity *aidos* (a sense
of shame; religious reverence) and *dike* (justice in judgment;
respect for the rights of others) in order to cope with the social
pressures of living with others. Oedipus arrives in a society
that expects of him these two virtues.

A philological insight often leads Vernant and his
colleagues into a structural analysis based on the varied
meanings of words. For example, Vernant portrays Oedipus as
a man caught in the ambiguities and reversals of his name. The
Greek word "oedipus" does mean "swollen foot," but also "I
know." Appropriately, Oedipus at once seeks self-knowledge
yet lives the ambiguities of the unbalanced or deviant life of
a cripple: "a superior and superhuman type of movement that
swings right around upon itself, describing a full circle, a type
of movement that the Greeks believed to be peculiar to a
number of exceptional categories of being."[7] Oedipus is
therefore off-balance, according to Vernant, and thus does not
have a balanced perspective of others. He desires self-
knowledge and is compelled to find it within the limitations of
his physical existence, even at the expense of his own family.

Those "others" include women. The philosophical
perception of otherness is a particularly attractive subject for
the structural method in that the alternation of sameness and
otherness provides a natural organizing principle which also
has functional ramifications. The situation of women in Greek
society is an abiding concern of the four leaders (Vernant,
Detienne, Vidal-Naquet, and Loraux) of the Gernet Center. In
the Sophoclean presentation of the Oedipus myth Merope,
Jocasta, Antigone, and the Sphinx embody the feminine
gender on stage. The Sphinx has a woman's face and represents
a major challenge to Oedipus in search of his identity as King
of Thebes. Gernet notes that it is through Oedipus' victory
over the Sphinx that he acquires his promised heritage: Jocasta
and Thebes.[8] However, Oedipus the riddle-solver, according
to Vidal-Naquet, is unable to solve the problem of his own
fate and relies on Merope, Jocasta, and Antigone to get him
through the three stages of his own life. In addition, it is Hera
who punishes Laius for refusing to have sex with his wife,

Jocasta. Hence the curse of a goddess rules the fate of Oedipus in a society where women have no citizenship and few legal rights. Loraux examines women's rights as mothers and human beings in roles played by Merope, Jocasta, and Antigone in Oedipus' life-cycle. Their fates offer commentaries on the social and political plight of women.

The Oedipus myth is a crucial story for French structuralism. On the one hand Lévi-Strauss identifies himself as a scientist who relies on the logical model of formal structures to decipher the substratum of myths. Despite the apparent randomness of myths, in which anything can happen, he insists that myths in fact have a rigid order, one which reflects the single way in which all humanity thinks—what Lévi-Strauss calls the "human spirit." Thus revealed, this human spirit leads politically to his ideal of a "dynamic tolerance" for all cultures, races, and ideologies. However, Lévi-Strauss' postulation of the autochthonous origins of Oedipus exemplifies what a contemporary anthropologist says about scientific pretensions: "serious scientific inquiry should not search for ultimate causes deriving from some outside source but must confine itself to the study of relations existing between facts which are directly accessible to observation."[9] Lévi-Strauss the scientist comes up short as he applies his skills to the Oedipus myth.

On the other hand Vernant and his colleagues do study the "relations existing between facts" and present Oedipus with both internal and external cohesion. Internal cohesion is achieved by explaining his character from within the myth. External cohesion comes with the cultural setting of Greece in the fourth and fifth centuries B.C. This view of myth focuses on the imaginative power of humanity to express itself analogically rather than univocally. Language is at the heart of understanding this myth as well as others. But the words must be understood in their context. Rather than the taxonomic categories of structural linguistics demonstrated by the diagrammatic analysis of Oedipus by Lévi-Strauss, philology offers the contextual power of being precise while also exposing the ambivalence of the language expressing Oedipus' evolving character. The humanity of Oedipus is at stake in the face of charges that he was born not of woman but of the earth. After all, myth is a product of the human imagination.

THE AMBIVALENCE AT THE CORE OF OEDIPUS

Lévi-Strauss' diagrammatic layout of the Oedipus myth into four columns is the model for his structuralist method. Lévi-Strauss arrives at these four columns by grouping together vertically similar events in the Oedipus myth. To read the chart[10] (translated on the next page), the events are to be read from left to right, column after column. This chart is supposed to render obvious the repetition of four hidden features in the myth. These four features—overrating and underrating of blood relations (columns 1 and 2); denial and persistence of autochthonous origins (columns 3 and 4)—create the structure of the myth by constituting two sets of contradictory features. The binary oppositions create an ambivalence at the core of the Oedipus myth. Overrating and underrating of blood relations are set off against the denial and the persistence of the autochthonous origins of man. Simply put, the Oedipus myth is the acting out of the struggle over human origins. Myth thus *invents* reality by postulating the validity of autochthonous origins. The tension in the Oedipus myth is thus created by the opposition of blood relations to autochthony. This view is in contrast to the functionalist view of the Gernet Center, which proposes myth as an *inverted mirror* of reality.

TO NEXT PAGE

The Oedipus Myth According to Lévi-Strauss

1	2	3	4
Cadmus seeks his sister Europa ravished by Zeus			
		Cadmus kills the dragon	
	The Spartoi kill one another		
			Labdacos (Laius' father) = "lame"
	Oedipus kills his father Laius		Laius (O.'s father) = "left-sided"
		Oedipus kills the Sphinx	
Oedipus marries his mother Jocasta			
	Eteocles kills his brother Polynices		Oedipus = "swollen-foot"
Antigone buries her brother Polynices against the interdiction			

OUT OF FORM CAME STRUCTURE

Vladimir Propp's *The Morphology of the Folktale* (1928) provides a classic "syntagmatic," or linear, model for myth analysis. He classifies thirty-one functions, specifically narrative acts, by which Russian folktales can be narrated sequentially. This model is "syntagmatic" (from the word "syntax") because it classifies the order of agents, acts, recipients, and other components of the plot. Lévi-Strauss regards such linear, sequential forms as obvious and superficial. Instead, he prefers a nonlinear, structural, "paradigmatic" (from the word "paradigm") analysis, in which the contradictions of linear models can be resolved semantically by polar oppositions such as that in the Oedipus myth between blood relations and autochthonous beings. He makes short shrift of Propp's syntagmatic analysis of form and focuses instead on structure: "Form is defined by opposition to content, an entity in its own right, but structure has no distinct content: it is content itself, and the logical organization in which it is arrested is conceived as a property of the real."[11] The structure partakes of polar categories which the "real" holds in logical contradiction such as male/female and life/death. Hence Lévi-Strauss posits the structure of myth as a logical means for setting the semantic parameters for contradictions outside the stories of the myths.

The horizontal and vertical axes serve Lévi-Strauss well in charting these contradictions. Once again, he learned this technique from Roman Jakobson, who claimed that a poem can be charted linguistically on a grid composed of six functions and two axes (the horizontal or syntagmatic axis and the vertical or paradigmatic axis) which trace the "duplex structure" of language.[12] The six functions are plotted somewhere along these axes and represent the addressor, message, addressee, context, code (common to addressor and addressee), and contact (physical and psychological connection).[13] For Lévi-Strauss, the semantic aspects of these functions are usually charted in such a way that binary relationships like those in the Oedipus myth between the overrating and the underrating of blood relations constitute the principal basis for his diagrams.

The resulting grid of the interlocking axes visually brings together a structure which is not apparent in the linear, horizontal, or syntagmatic unfolding of a myth. Where the literal sense of the story introduces simple contradictions, the structure resolves or diminishes them. Lévi-Strauss admits that these contradictions are his point of entry into myths: he seeks "to try and find an order behind this apparent disorder."[14] The Spartite episode of the Cadmus myth, for example, implies that the Thebans were born from the earth. This story jars with the great crime of incest committed by Oedipus. Did, then, Oedipus really come from the earth or from his mother Jocasta? Why the ambivalence of Oedipus' ancestral origins? In response to this apparent disorder, Lévi-Strauss looks for a vertical layering of truth because the horizontal or literal telling of the myth does not provide any answers.

This vertical layering is by direct inspiration from Marxism, psychoanalysis, and geology -- the three influences that in *Tristes Tropiques* Lévi-Strauss calls the "mistresses" of his ethnological career. Marxism argues that beneath the surface superstructure of politics lies hidden a deeper substructure. Politics becomes the class struggle to get beyond the appearances of what a dominant class projects as the values of a society. For Lévi-Strauss, who is not a committed Marxist, the lesson of the class struggle seething beneath the appearances of a society is instructive in his appreciation of the setting for myth. Struggle is at the core of mythic structure. The Oedipus myth displays the tension between blood and earth origins which, like Marxism, reveals the struggle of the deep structure hidden beneath the contradictions in the apparent story.

Similarly, psychoanalysis provides Lévi-Strauss with insight into myths. Psychoanalysis reveals the unconscious, or latent, sources of conscious, or manifest, behavior. Once again, there is suspicion of the validity of the obvious and a tendency to look for "reality" somewhere other than on the surface. Psychoanalysis explains abnormal, or illogical, behavior through the probing of the unconscious. For Lévi-Strauss, the analysis of myth is a search for a structure which can logically explain an apparent contradiction. That search is "for the invariant, or for the invariant elements among superficial differences."[15] While an "invariant" is something which remains the same in the course of the changing events in a myth, a pattern of invariants reveals a myth's structure. For example, the autochthonous and blood relations are invariant elements buried in the Oedipus myth. The fourfold structures he identifies (overrating and underrating blood relations; denial and persistence of autochthonous origins) are similar to the childhood events that psychoanalysts discover to explain behavior in adults. In both cases there are hidden explanations about the origins of human behavior that must be exposed in order to understand the whole story of a person—what Lévi-Strauss calls the structure of the human spirit.

Geology likewise abets Lévi-Strauss' analysis of myth. As geology discovers layers of sediment from previous historical periods in a paradigmatic fashion by exposing layers superimposed one on the other, so Lévi-Strauss probes the surface of myths to discover other layers besides the horizontal one represented by the literal narration of the story. Often there are many interwoven layers, as with the fourfold structure representing the denial or acquiescence of autochthonous or blood relations. In geology a core sample reveals multiple layers of historical events. In myth an invariant element in the narrative such as the autochthonous origin of man provides access to a discussion of its layered components like the four features of human origins in the Oedipus story.

The three models of vertical layering also entail historical visions. Marxism advocates respect for history in its method of dialectical materialism, whereby an individual is engaged in the class struggle of the moment with all its economic and ideological values. Psychoanalysis explains present behavior by reference to past events—dreams, habits, and relationships. Geology focuses on the residue of the past in the present.

Yet Lévi-Strauss often opposes his structuralist method to history. History is the use of chronological sequence, similar to the horizontal or syntactical axis, to ground a reading in its literal event as a speech act. Although he is ordinarily reluctant to give history a place in structuralism, he does demonstrate in the Asdiwal analysis that "only historical development permits weighing and evaluating the components of the present in their respective relationships."[16] Oddly enough, that analysis is not repeated in his later work, which returns to the earlier, ahistorical method.

The ahistorical method is partly grounded in an idiosyncratic model of the "bricoleur," or the resourceful inventor. In an almost classic counterpart to the opposition of *logos* (reason) to *muthos* (the mythic imagination) in ancient Greek mentality, the bricoleur is contrasted to the engineer. While *logos* theoretically overcame *muthos* as the Greek city-state evolved, the bricoleur of mythical thought continues to dominate the engineer, imprisoned by the compromises of techniques to science. Similarly, Lévi-Strauss contrasts the movement of myth to that of history with its ideological commitment to chronological time as a touchstone of truth:

> Mythical thought for its part is imprisoned in the events and experiences which it never tires of ordering and re-ordering in its search to find them a meaning. But it also acts as a liberator by its protest against the idea that anything can be meaningless with which science at first resigned itself to a compromise.[17]

The bricoleur is thus a model for analyzing the contradictions in myth because invention and resourcefulness are needed to explore the logical bases, the semantic reasons, for the apparent non sequiturs. Lévi-Strauss believes that one has to move vertically when the horizontal path is blocked.

THE HERMENEUTIC CRISIS

A vertical, or paradigmatic, reading of myth incorporates symbols, the objects used to represent abstractions, in the literal story. Hermeneutics, the discipline of interpreting a text and explaining that meaning to others, is similarly attracted to the symbolic explanations of myths. Paul Ricoeur, the hermeneutic philosopher who takes exception to Lévi-Strauss' structuralist readings of myth, contends that "the myth should be subordinated to the symbol."[18] He means that myths refer to an external system of *conscious*, not hidden, religious values, of which the symbol is a part. Ricoeur later includes the methods of Lévi-Strauss in the hermeneutic scheme by stipulating that Lévi-Strauss explains the mechanics of myth while he, Ricoeur, interprets the meaning.[19] For Ricoeur, the structure of the Oedipus myth revolves around whether God created humanity from the earth or whether there was an original Mother Deity from which human life emanated. Ricoeur thus adds the dimensions of theological meaning and teleological vision to the structuralist approach.

For Lévi-Strauss, there are symbols in myths. Their significance has to do with what Lévi-Strauss calls the universality of the human mind (*l'esprit humain*). Symbols appear to work similarly in myths. Lévi-Strauss cites the example of the autochthonous theme in Oedipus as occurring also in Zuni and Pueblo myths about human origins. These similar symbols exemplify what Lévi-Strauss calls "internal homologies."[20] "Homology," a term taken from biology, means the repetition of a similar structure. For Lévi-Strauss, homology is internal because the symbol becomes a reflection of similar patterns in human thinking.

Ricoeur accuses Lévi-Strauss here of manipulating a "Kantian unconscious"[21] with the theory of internal homologies. Since the Idealist philosopher Immanuel Kant (1724-1804) speculated that there is a spirit ruling over the world in protective fashion to ensure a whole rather than fragmentation, the reference portrays Lévi-Strauss as having a model for human thinking before he actually discovers anything among myths. Despite Lévi-Strauss' penchant for the materialism of Marxism and the scientific method of the anthropologist, he claims to be flattered, not offended, by the association with Kant. Kant was the inspiration for the Enlightenment adaptation of reason and the beginnings of modern science. Moreover, Kant's categorical imperative, by which an individual's behavior is governed by the same principles as the behavior of the individual's class, is similar to the internal homologies by which the structure of one myth is sometimes explained by the similarity to the structures of other myths. Lévi-Strauss' explanation for the structure of the Oedipus myth is substantiated through analogy to other myths which likewise explain human origins with the pairing of autochthonous and maternal births. The hermeneutic reference to external symbolic systems is especially foreign to Lévi-Strauss' portrayal of the integrity of myths. His task is not to recover what an author of a myth had to say. Instead, Lévi-Strauss would have the myths think for themselves. Indeed, in his four-volume *Mythologiques* (1964-71) he analyzes the thinking process "taking place in the myths, in their reflection upon themselves and their interrelation."[22] The rejection of the external symbolic reference becomes ever more curious whenever Lévi-Strauss identifies the inspiration for anthropology in the natural sciences.[23] The empirical methods of the natural sciences should ground the symbols of myths in such external systems as the rituals, ceremonies, and totemic artifacts of various cultures. Yet his method is in fact more akin to philosophy or to ideology than to science. The unity in human thought that he postulates is never proved scientifically. As an ethnologist, he collects many myths and relates them. But the myths are all related in different fashions. Engineering, as representative of the sciences, is contrasted to bricolage, the resourceful ingenuity, of myths. In engineering, knowledge is the systematic tracking of truth through the application of formal logic. By contrast, in bricolage, one sign leads to another sign[24] playfully erasing its predecessor—as exemplified in the oral myths he selects, where no source can be assigned to discover what the author was trying to communicate.

THE REFUSAL OF THE EXISTENTIAL DIALECTIC

As we have seen, Lévi-Strauss' focus on internal structure precludes history. Jean-Paul Sartre, who advocates the struggle with historical factors as recognition that the human situation entails decisions about commitment to others, denounces the Lévi-Straussian method for its lack of historical dialectic.[25] Lévi-Strauss claims that Marxism has been one of his handmaidens. He even insists that the binary tensions he finds in myths are developments of the dialectic he learned from Marxism. However, the Marxist Sartre objects to the facile equation of binary with dialectic. The dialectic is an involved response to the situation of a given people or tribe among whom the myths continue to be narrated because of the group's meaning for the myths. The meanings that Lévi-Strauss discovers are not connected either to the peoples who narrate the myths or to their listeners. The Sartrean view of the dialectic is more closely emulated by Vernant and his colleagues.

Lévi-Strauss identifies his structuralist presentation of myth as a "totalizing" enterprise. By totalizing he means that his method is not focused by the teleological vision of a single philosophical or ideological position such as existentialism. Instead, he is concerned with "a total understanding: if you don't understand everything, you don't explain anything ... [about] this totalitarian ambition of the savage mind."[26] This ambitious prospectus often provides analogies between what he calls the "system" of myth and the systems of language and music. By system he means a closed network of communication within which structures have specific functions in linking the levels of meaning. In language there is a three-level paradigm linking phonemes (basic units of sound producing meaning), words, and sentences. By contrast, myths lack the equivalent of phonemes but do have words and sentences. Music has counterparts to phonemes and sentences but not to words. By matching and contrasting these three systems, Lévi-Strauss strives to learn more about the totality of myth as a system of communication.

The Russian linguist Nikolai Troubetskoy provided the model in the early 1930s for phonemic analysis. He discovered that phonemes are context-sensitive. Lévi-Strauss seeks to explain why the narrative contexts of myths preclude the counterparts to phonemes in language. Early in his career he pondered the existence of mythemes, basic units of myths translatable from one myth to another. However, his abstractions from the myths produce the structures rather than the basic constituents from which the words and sentences of myths are composed. Marcel Detienne, a Hellenist by interest and a philologist by training, especially objects to the Oedipus myth as an example of the totalizing system of myths because of Lévi-Strauss' assumption of "a chain of relations, a succession of concepts, a system of signifying oppositions distributed on different planes, at various semantic levels."[27] The analysis of the Asdiwal myth is an example of how Lévi-Strauss implements such a totalizing vision for myth.

THE ETHNOGRAPHIC CONTEXT

Lévi-Strauss gives an exceptional example of the "ethnographic context" in his structuralist analysis of a North American Indian myth. First published in 1958, "The Story of Asdiwal" ("Le Geste d'Asdiwal") is reprinted in the second volume of his *Structural Anthropology*. The chief distinguishing features of this presentation are the geographical, sociological, economic, and cosmological settings for the Tsimshian and Nisqa Indian tribes who invented this myth. The four versions of the myth, three Tsimshian and one Nisqa, were collected by the American anthropologist Franz Boas at the turn of the century. The Tsimshian and Nisqa Indians inhabit the Nass and Skeena River Valleys of British Columbia just south of Alaska. They are matrilineal (kinship determined by the mother) tribes with patrilocal (living with the father) families. The Tsimshian rely primarily upon candlefish and salmon for food. Because the Skeena River freezes, they are driven seasonally by periods of severe famine to roam toward the Nass River Valley, where the Nisqa live in villages year round. Lévi-Strauss, who himself provides this setting, claims that the setting is related "dialectically" to the Indian tribes because the details of the story are not simply mimetic reflections of the lives of the peoples in the area. Instead, the ethnographic setting stands in a particular relationship to the peoples' lives. Let us look at the myth itself before considering Lévi-Strauss' analysis. It is winter in the Skeena valley, and famine reigns. A mother and a daughter, both widows because of the food crisis and separated because of their marriages, decide to meet midway up the river. The mother heads eastward and the daughter westward. During their meeting a stranger, Hatsenas ("bird of good omen"), appears; provides food for the women; and marries the younger one, who gives birth to Asdiwal ("crosser of mountains," "to be in danger," and a name for a thunderbird). The father gives Asdiwal equipment with magical powers to overcome the trials of life. One day a white she-bear lures Asdiwal to the home of its father, the sun. Asdiwal marries the bear's sister, the Evening Star. The couple descend to earth, where Asdiwal has an affair with a woman from his village. Evening Star leaves him, and Asdiwal marries the daughter of a village chief. Her brothers argue with Asdiwal over the respective merits of sea hunters and mountain hunters. Asdiwal demonstrates himself a superior hunter. The brothers take their sister and abandon Asdiwal. Four other brothers, also sea hunters, meet Asdiwal at the River Nass, where he also meets and marries their sister. Asdiwal and his brothers-in-law go hunting on the sea. A storm comes up and sweeps Asdiwal onto a rock from which he is rescued by a mouse who takes him to the subterranean home of the sea lions. Returning home to his wife and son, he longs to return home to the Skeena Valley. However, he forgets his magic snowshoes and dies stranded on the mountains, where he is turned into stone.

Lévi-Strauss notes that this myth has very little value as a documentary source for the lives of the Tsimshian and Nisqa Indians. He thus rejects the claims for myth as a historical record. Lévi-Strauss, not the myth, provides details about the lives of the tribes. In this way Lévi-Strauss sets up a series of contradictions both within the story and within the actual lives of the narrators. These binary oppositions provide the bases for diagrams, or "schemata," of four levels on which the story can be generated by a series of unresolved oppositions. These four levels are the geographic, the techno-economic, the sociological, and the cosmological. Lévi-Strauss discovers that the story has a series of unresolved oppositions between low and high, earth and heaven, man and woman, endogamy and exogamy, mountain and sea hunting, and land and water. The contradictions are resolved by analogy to the system of music:

> But these sequences are organized on planes at different levels of abstraction in accordance with schemata, which exist simultaneously, superimposed one upon the other; just as a melody composed for several voices is held within bounds by two-dimensional constraints: first by its own melodic line, which is horizontal, and second by the contrapuntal schemata, which are vertical.[28]

Through this explanation of the different levels in the Asdiwal myth Lévi-Strauss is able to demonstrate the "contrapuntal" resolution of its contradictions in the symmetrical patterns that form the structure of the story.

In his analysis of the Asdiwal myth, rather than proceeding from a myth to a culture, Lévi-Strauss does the reverse. He enriches the understanding of the contradictions within a myth by reference to the cultural context. For example, the exogamous marriages of the Tsimshian are questioned by the presentation of an Asdiwal who cannot succeed in marriage, despite his three attempts to marry outside his clan. Asdiwal must go off alone to find peace in his homeland. These unsuccessful marriages are also linked to the matrilineal but patrilocal familial structure of the Tsimshians. Although power passes through the mother, the family lives with the father, who is probably driven far from home in his search for food. Asdiwal provides a "dialectical" model for the Tsimshian men, who are fishermen. He is a mountain hunter and has magical powers to help him succeed. It is the sea which threatens him and maroons him on a rock, where he is rescued by a lowly female mouse. Yet she is female—the source of continuity and family, according to the Tsimshian. Asdiwal roamed to the Nass River, as do the Tsimshian seasonally. However, he was more resourceful as a mountain hunter and could ascend (to the sun) and descend (to the world of the sea lions) rather than merely roam east-west or north-south, as did the Tsimshians. Asdiwal is thus a mythical hero who incarnates the duality of life in Northern British Columbia:

> Everything seems to suggest that, as it draws to its close, the apparent narrative (the sequences) tends to approach the latent content of the myth (the schemata). It is a convergence which is not unlike that which the listener discovers in the final chords of a symphony.[29]

As the conductor of a symphony, Lévi-Strauss is also obligated to encompass the four divergent versions within his reading of Asdiwal. Once again, it is a mythical world drawing the outside world into itself and its structures. The life experiences of the Tsimshian and Nisqa Indians serve to provide Lévi-Strauss with the information to constitute his paradigm for the Asdiwal myth. The relationship of ethnographic context to myth is a closely knit one.

The analysis of Asdiwal remains an anomaly among Lévi-Strauss' analyses. Fittingly, it is the one that inspired the contextualist school of myth analysis. Marcel Detienne, who objects to Lévi-Strauss' indifference to context in his reading of Oedipus, recommends the Asdiwal model to classicists. The other influences of Lévi-Strauss on the contextualists have been largely terminological. For example, Nicole Loraux uses Lévi-Strauss' autochthonous origins, homology, and totemism.

NOTES

1. Claude Lévi-Strauss, *Anthropologie structurale*, I (Paris: Plon, 1958), pp. 239-43.

2. Claude Lévi-Strauss, *Myth and Meaning* (New York: Shocken, 1979), p. 40.

3. René Girard, "Système du délire," *Critique*, XXVIII, 306 (November 1972), 976. My translation of: "La psychanalyse n'a pas à inventer l'Oedipe, disent-ils [Deleuze and Guattari], les sujets se présentent chez leurs psychiatres déjà tout oedipianisé."

4. Lowell Edmunds, *Oedipus: The Ancient Legend and its Later Analogues* (Baltimore: Johns Hopkins University Press, 1985), p. 47. Edmunds catalogues seventy-six analogues of the Oedipus myth narrated in thirty-one languages ranging from Albanian to Zulu.

5. Lévi-Strauss, *Anthropologie structurale*, p. 240: "par l'ensemble de toutes ses versions."

6. *Ibid.*, p. 180.

7. Jean-Pierre Vernant, "The Lame Tyrant," in Vernant and Pierre Vidal-Naquet, *Myth and Tragedy in Ancient Greece*, tr. Janet Lloyd (New York: Zone, 1988), p. 210.

8. Louis Gernet and André Boulanger, *Le Génie grec dans la religion* (Paris: Albin Michel, 1932), p. 77.

9. Edmund Leach, *Genesis as Myth and Other Essays* (London: Jonathan Cape, 1971), p. 86.

10. Lévi-Strauss, *Anthropologie structurale*, p. 236.

11. Claude Lévi-Strauss, "Structure and Form," tr. Monique Layton, in Ariadna and Richard Martin, ed., *Theory and History of Folklore* (Minneapolis: University of Minnesota Press, 1984), p. 167.

12. Roman Jakobson, "Shifters, Verbal Categories, and the Russian Verb," in his *Selected Writings*, vol. 1 (The Hague: Mouton, 1962), p. 150.

13. Roman Jakobson, "Linguistics and Poetics," in *Style in Language*, ed. Thomas A. Sebeok (Cambridge: MIT Press, 1960), p. 353.

14. Lévi-Strauss, *Myth and Meaning*, p. 11.

15. *Ibid.*, p. 8.

16. Lévi-Strauss, *Anthropologie structurale*, p. 17.

17. Claude Lévi-Strauss, *The Savage Mind*, tr. not given (Chicago: University of Chicago Press, 1966), p. 22.

18. Paul Ricoeur, *The Conflict of Interpretations*, tr. Don Ihde (Evanston: Northwestern University Press, 1974), p. 28.

19. I thank Robert Segal for explaining the later inclusion of Lévi-Strauss into Ricoeur's analysis of meaning.

20. Claude Lévi-Strauss, *Totemism*, tr. Rodney Needham (Boston: Beacon Press, 1963), p. 78.

21. Paul Ricoeur, "Structure et herméneutique," *Esprit*, XXI, 332 (November 1963), 600.

22. Claude Lévi-Strauss, *The Raw and the Cooked*, tr. John and Doreen Weightman (New York: Harper & Row, 1969), p. 12.

23. See the discussion of this scientific claim by Lévi-Strauss in Mireille Marc-Lipiansky, *Le Structuralisme de Lévi-Strauss* (Paris: Payot, 1973), pp. 240ff.

24. See my essay "The Semiotics of Lévi-Strauss: Communication as Translation," in *The Semiotic Web—1989*, ed. Thomas A. Sebeok (New York: Mouton de Gruyter, 1990), pp. 61–88, for a discussion of Lévi-Strauss' model for myths as a source of semiotic research.

25. Jean-Paul Sartre, *Critique de la raison dialectique* (Paris: Gallimard, 1960), p. 104ff. For a discussion of the stakes in the Sartre/Lévi-Strauss debate see Lawrence Rosen, "Language, History, and the Logic of Inquiry in Lévi-Strauss and Sartre," *History and Theory*, X, 3 (1971), 290ff.

26. Lévi-Strauss, *Myth and Meaning*, p. 17.

27. Marcel Detienne, *Dionysos Slain*, tr. Mireille and Leonard Muellner (Baltimore: Johns Hopkins University Press, 1979), p. 7.

28. Claude Lévi-Strauss, "The Story of Asdiwal," in his *Structural Anthropology*, vol. 2, tr. Monique Layton (New York: Basic Books, 1976), p. 161.

29. *Ibid.*, p. 165.

Chapter Four

VERNANT: A LOGIC OF THE EQUIVOCAL

Of all the various forms of structuralism that he has inspired, Lévi-Strauss feels closest to that of Jean-Pierre Vernant and his colleagues at the Gernet Center.[1] However, the word "structuralism" brings with it a *Weltanschauung*—an "ideology" as the Indo-European mythologist Georges Dumézil would call it—that Vernant does not accept. The "ideology" entails linguistic theories derived from Ferdinand de Saussure and applied to a "structuralist" agenda principally by Barthes, Lévi-Strauss, the philosopher and historian of ideas Michel Foucault (1926-1984), the psychoanalyst Jacques Lacan (1901-1981), and the Marxian philosopher Louis Althusser (1918-1990).[2]

Vernant's disavowal of "structuralism" stems from his own penchant for avoiding controversy, especially in the wake of the hostile reception by classicists to Lévi-Strauss' reading of the Oedipus myth. Although Vernant has been evenhanded in his appraisal of Lévi-Strauss' "structuralist" approach to myths, he prefers to be distinguished for using "structural analysis"[3] in combination with a contextualist approach to myth. He characterizes his approach as contextualist as well as structuralist. In a 1966 conference on structuralism at Johns Hopkins Vernant identified context as the situation whereby "every message implies a necessary complicity between the interlocutor and his audience."[4] Without making specific references to the survivalist views of myth by Barthes and Lévi-Strauss, Vernant elaborated his own position on the context of myth by identifying the "semantic fields" of law, religion, and politics. These semantic fields or contexts are bundles of meanings understood differently by both the interlocutor and the audience of myths. By precisely identifying which meanings are pertinent to either the interlocutor or the audience, Vernant provides a logic for the contradictions in myths. Meaning can vary because of the context of a myth. Rather than visually presenting a diagram for the binary structures of contradictions or of the variances in meanings, as Lévi-Strauss is wont to do, Vernant describes the situations in which equivocation is valued by the Greeks. Although trained as a philosopher, Vernant labeled himself a historian in approaching this notion of context and its relationship to structural analysis.

Jean-Pierre Vernant has long concentrated on the area of the rising Greek city-states. He takes a special interest in the 6th century B.C., when the Greek tradition of *logos*, a tendency to use philosophical discourse in the discussion of cultural issues, began to distinguish itself from *muthos*, the narratives of the gods intervening in human affairs. At the same time the Greek city-states were evolving. This situation arose just after the popularity of the theatrical genre of tragedy, specifically as practiced by Aeschylus and Sophocles, which continued for about one hundred years. *Oedipus Rex* especially enjoyed a receptive audience in the early fifth century (c. 420 B.C.). Within this setting Vernant sets out to answer the same question time and again: "What is the link between the semantic space revealed by structural analysis as the myth's intellectual framework and the sociohistorical context in which the myth was produced?"[5] By "semantic space" Vernant means the significance attributed to concepts such as justice, cunning intelligence, the home, among others in a given framework, that is, the myth or story about the Greek setting for the given concept. Each myth groups together interwoven concepts crucial to the city-state and to the lives of the Greeks. This grouping is "the semantic space" in which equivocation, or ambivalence, governs. In fifth century Greece the Sophists, itinerant teachers, did not abandon the fabulous *muthos* in favor of the discursive advantages of of *logos*: "the tension remains: the contradictions are not overcome and cannot be .... There is not yet any Aristotelian logic because, for the Sophists, one discourse is as good as the other."[6] Although Vernant respects this attitude toward ambivalence, he does have a logical method to present the integration of semantic space in the sociohistorical context of myths. By contrast, Lévi-Strauss prefers to ignore the context in favor of cross-cultural, cognitive categories which point to common ways of thinking.

Vernant's method supplements the grid used by Lévi-Strauss. Vernant identifies three components in a text: the syntax or logic, the semantic content, and the structural context or the structure of its intellectual world.[7] The first two components are basically the same as the syntagmatic and paradigmatic axes of Lévi-Strauss. The third dimension is the expansion of the semantic content into discussions of the relationships between myth and its audience or interlocutor. The semantic fields are similar to Lévi-Strauss' setting for the Asdiwal myth in economics, geography, social and familial history, and cosmology. Whereas the Asdiwal setting did not address the myth as written document, the semantic fields represent meanings of a written culture which survives as the work of plural documents, effectively providing a chorus about the nature of the semantic fields in which the written myth occurs. For Vernant, these semantic fields are likewise diverse disciplines which specify the uniqueness of the heritage within which a written myth occurs. He has collaborated with Marcel Detienne on several projects in which philology is the central organizing semantic field around which can be explained an individual myth and whole mythologies—collections of myths brought together for a specific purpose, as with Hesiod's *Theogony*. The words *mètis* ("cunning intelligence") and *oikos* ("familial territory"), for example, are explored for their special meanings in the myths of the Greeks and provide rich commentaries on the cultures which valued these concepts in varying ways over time.

In his expansion of the semantics of Greek myths Vernant has a vision of the spatial organization of the structure of the Greek intellectual world. He has a special affinity for geometry and the implications for the organization of space on Greek culture and its myths. For example, just as the new political idea of equality (*isonomia*: "equilibrium") is presented by Vernant as implying a geometrical view of the city with the egalitarian, symmetrical, and reversible forum as its center, so the myth of Hestia, goddess of the hearth, implies a static view of family and territory associated with the central place in the home of the hearth as *oikos* and Hestia's sacred place. Thus for Vernant the context is a cultural, spatial, and cultural index which expands upon the horizontal and vertical axes of Lévi-Strauss' semantic interpretations.

ARBITRARY CHOICES

In his overview of myth analysis[8] Vernant singles out Lévi-Strauss as the key structuralist. Vernant does not mention Barthes although the subtitle of his essay "Myth Today" makes an allusion to Barthes that most French readers of Vernant could not miss. The essay presents three kinds of contemporary myth analysis: symbolism (e.g., Ernst Cassirer), functionalism (e.g., Bronislaw Malinowski), and structuralism (e.g., Lévi-Strauss). Vernant focuses on the structuralism of Lévi-Strauss after acknowledging that "the most spectacular progress in contemporary mythological research has been made by the anthropologists and ethnologists rather than by Greek scholars."[9] Like his classicist colleagues, Vernant finds Lévi-Strauss rather arbitrary in his choice of the Oedipus myth and his selection of phrases for the "mythemes" around which the semantic structure of the myth is organized. In addition, Vernant objects to the implication by Lévi-Strauss that any myth may be used as a tool for the logical resolution of unsolvable contradictions in life. For Vernant, the use of any myth by outsiders violates the place of that myth within its own semantic fields. Each myth has a specific function within its culture. To appropriate the myths of others, without consideration for the values that are attributed to these myths, is an act of aggression against the originating culture.

Vernant introduces his variant of "structural analysis," which I call the Contextualist School, as the basis for the

Center for the Comparative Study of Ancient Societies at the Ecole Pratique des Hautes Études in Paris during the mid-1970s. It was Pierre Vidal-Naquet who, as Vernant's successor as Director of the Center, had the Center named after Louis Gernet in 1989. Vernant clearly distinguishes his interest in myth from that of Lévi-Strauss. Lévi-Strauss focuses on oral myths, which generally come from "cold," primitive societies, in which time is not stressed, rather than on "hot societies," which have written myths and have come to grips with history. Vernant thinks that both written and oral myths ought to be subject to myth analysis. He prefers to separate written myths from oral myths because written myths are "governed by more varied and adaptable rules than oral composition of the formulaic type."[10] In addition, a written myth allows for a more rigorous, more strictly ordered analysis than an oral myth. Vernant is concerned with the changes made on myths once they become written. For Lévi-Strauss, the distinction appears to have no importance. In this spirit, Vernant especially concentrates on the transposition of written myth into tragedy, a specific literary form practiced by the Greeks during the fifth and sixth centuries B.C. Although Lévi-Strauss focuses on an originally oral myth—Oedipus—that was transposed into written form by no less than Hesiod, Homer, Aeschylus, and Sophocles, the French ethnologist does not specify a single written version and instead insists upon using all the variants of the myth. In effect, he makes the Oedipus myth into an oral tradition known by all and not limited to a single written document. He even includes Freud's interpretation as just another variant of the myth itself.

Vernant, however, presents the *tragedy* of Oedipus as a written version of myth. We are reminded that Sophocles, Euripides (*Phoenician Women*), and Aeschylus (*Oedipus*) added details such as Oedipus' exile and his death to Homer's version, which portrays Oedipus dying as King of Thebes. Those details not only enrich the myth but provide specific examples of the changes in the story. Lévi-Strauss chooses which details conform to his presentation from any version of the Oedipus myth while ignoring the differences in the variants. Vernant's training as historian and philologist helps him realize that "there is no such thing as myth in the untouched state."[11] He is intent upon recognizing the diversity of each variant whereas Lévi-Strauss seeks only similarities. One key distinction made by Vernant is the difference between myth and mythology. As opposed to a single, unconnected story, or myth, a mythology is a unified, interconnected group of stories with internal coherence. Similalry, Lévi-Strauss sought internal coherence among myths that led him to the theory of a single human spirit represented by mythology. Vernant, however, maintains that each variant of a myth must be placed within its distinctive mythology, which gives the myth its meaning. Vernant compares a mythology with a philosophy because of the rigor and complexity of both. The myth of Oedipus has belonged to various mythologies (e.g., those of Homer and Hesiod) in its many variants. Therefore Vernant separates his approach from that of Lévi-Strauss on the issue of looking only for similarities: "if synonymity is the rule, then mythology in all its diversity can no longer be regarded as a system with meaning."[12]

Vernant agrees with Lévi-Strauss that myths have *both* surface and underlying meanings. He acknowledges that Lévi-Strauss has brought "a turning point and a new departure"[13] to myth analysis. Vernant concurs with Lévi-Strauss in his refutation of the Freudian reading as misguided. However, Vernant gives different reasons. For Lévi-Strauss, Freud erred in limiting Oedipus to the model for the triangulation of the family. For Vernant, Freud was not historically oriented enough and thus distorted the myth.

Vernant wants to use Lévi-Strauss' Asdiwal analysis as a model with its "precise and exhaustive knowledge of the myth's cultural and ethnographical context."[14] With this model in mind, Vernant returns to the Oedipus myth in order to apply his knowledge of the Greek ethnographic context to Lévi-Strauss' comments on the generational patterns in the Oedipus myth. Lévi-Strauss is the first to have pointed out the physical similarities in three generations of Labdacids down through Oedipus. All three—Labdacos, Laius, and Oedipus—share a common destiny of lameness: a lopsided gait, the lack of symmetry between the two sides of the body, and a defect in one foot.[15] This remark is a key for Vernant in unlocking the intellectual code peculiar to the Oedipus myth.

OEDIPUS WITHOUT THE COMPLEX MASK

Vernant's Oedipus is an expansion of the four mythemes presented by Lévi-Strauss. Those four mythemes are manifestations of the four poles among which the myth oscillates: for and against human birth, for and against chthonic origins. For Vernant, ambivalence is also the primary structure of the Oedipus myth, especially in its application to Greek tragedies. Vernant does not, however, portray the ambivalence in as neatly diagrammatic a fashion as does Lévi-Strauss. The contexts of law, religion, and philosophy help explain Vernant's view of the ambivalence in the character Oedipus, discussed primarily in three essays of *Myth and Tragedy in Ancient Greece*.[16] Vernant introduces two Greek historical practices that played a crucial role in the tragic variations of the Oedipus myth: the *pharmakos*, or scapegoat ritual, and the practice of ostracism. The scapegoat ritual has been extensively discussed within the context of Judeo-Christian culture by the Franco-American scholar René Girard (b. 1923),[17] who presents the scapegoat as the victim of the communal human practice of triangulated desire. For Vernant, the institution of the scapegoat as a Greek custom at about the same time as tragedy helps explain Oedipus' banishment and suicide in Sophocles' tragic trilogy. In addition, the practice of ostracism, voted by a majority of the Greek parliament, made the scapegoat ritual into a vehicle for ridding a community of a political threat.

These historical items contribute to what Vernant calls his method of historical psychology, adapted from his psychologist colleague at the Ecole pratique, Ignace Meyerson.[18] This method is offered as an alternative to the Freudian analysis of myth as the expression of a psychological complex. The

Oedipus complex was proposed by Freud to explain the triangular relationship of mother, father, and child. Freud had read Sophocles. He applied his reading of the myth to the case of a child's attachment to the parent of the opposite sex and hostility to the other parent. Vernant agrees with Lévi-Strauss that Freud's comments on the Oedipus myth constitute a new variant of the myth rather than an interpretation of the myth. Freud's interpretation is not sufficiently contextual for Vernant. Freud, for example, derives the meaning of the Oedipus myth from the emotions that the play arouses in the spectators. Freud would have us believe that "by killing his father and marrying his mother, Oedipus is fulfilling a childhood desire of our own that we strive to forget."[19] However, Vernant maintains that the Oedipus in the tragedy does not manifest an "Oedipus complex" because he does not show any feelings at all toward Jocasta. According to Vernant, "if Oedipus had an Oedipus complex it would have been in his relationship to his first mother [Merope]."[20] Vernant believes that a psychoanalytic view of the myth distorts rather than illuminates our understanding of the myth. Historical psychology, by contrast, combines the best of two disciplines to help portray the ambivalence at the heart of the tragic rendition of the Oedipus myth.

For Vernant, the riddle is at the center of the Oedipus myth. Oedipus, the solver of riddles, cannot solve the riddle of his own identity. Hence there is ambivalence at the core of the myth. The very name "Oedipus" can be philologically linked to a riddle because of its two possible root meanings, or etymons: the Greek *oida* ("I know") and *pous* ("foot"). The linking of these two etymons in the person of Oedipus leads to a tension that is both intellectual and physiological. Oedipus is driven to know his true identity while hobbled by his lameness, itself part of both his heritage and his damnation because the lame Labdacos and the clumsy, left-handed Laius are part of the indication that the Labdacid genus will not be perpetuated. As Oedipus stubbornly pursues more and more complete self-knowledge, he is also realizing the physiological fate of the limp which makes him exceptional and increases the likelihood of his being ostracized as a scapegoat. The scapegoat ritual (*pharmakos*) was an annual event in Athens in which a parade was held to purify men and women through the identification of two scapegoats. Likewise the political institution of ostracism was invented at the end of the 6th century B.C. and entailed a ten-year temporary exile.

As Vernant seeks an explanation for the origin of tragedies and especially the tragic alteration of Oedipus on the Sophoclean stage, the combination of the *pharmakos* and the ostracism ritual help explain the additional details added by Sophocles. In the Sophoclean tragedies Oedipus' exile and subsequent suicide become significant additions explained by the social threat of the ambivalence in his condition. By focusing on the work of the Sophoclean tragedies of Oedipus, Vernant brings his own detailed knowledge of the historical setting to explain the ambivalent riddle at the center of the tragic myth of Oedipus as savior and assassin, divine king and tyrant, father of the land and criminal, and finally the promise of a new royal family and a curse fulfilled in that very family. The contradictions are the results of Oedipus' constant questioning to find out who he is, and ironically they constitute paradoxes that society cannot bear to maintain. In the period when *logos* was evolving and *muthos* was increasingly disparaged, Oedipus became a scapegoat and had to commit suicide. The need of Greek society for reasonable solutions precluded the ambivalent presentations of myths.

Greek tragedy appeared at about the same time that the city-state and its laws were being established and debated. This historical coincidence affects the presentation of Oedipus on the Greek stage. The riddle of Oedipus' name has its parallel in the structure of the tragedy, which for Vernant is also a riddle in its presentation, development, and resolution.[21] That very riddle unwinding on stage was a mirror of the political setting of Greek society as it evolved away from religious myths and toward rational, philosophical systems for its social models. The stage anticipated the forum as a setting for presenting the human drama of politics. Once the legal apparatus was formally in place in Greece, tragedy gradually decreased in popularity as politics favored the discursive techniques of *logos* and belittled *muthos* as a fanciful product of the religious imagination. Human law replaced divine law as the guiding principle for human conduct. The divine riddle gave way to a human discussion of compromise and equilibrium, a heritage that Athens obtained from its mythical origins which could not be rejected:

> And when Athena establishes the Council of the Judges on Areopagus, she repeats this theme, word for word. In establishing this rule as the imperative which her city must obey, the goddess emphasizes that the good is situated between two extremes, the City being based on a difficult accord between opposing powers which must find an equilibrium without destroying each other.[22]

While Greek tragedy was popular, Oedipus represented the lameness of the political system to find the means to legislate that accord. The ambivalence of Oedipus, as Vernant portrays him, extends to the lineage, marriage, power, and destiny of the Greeks also caught in trying to work out the relationships with what they knew about law and how they could reasonably implement it.

Through the methods of historical psychology, Vernant gives us an Oedipus also caught in the throes of his own duplicitous name. In seeking self-knowledge (*oida*) and a grounding for his lameness ("swollen foot": *oidos*; *pous*), he is representative of the rational society favoring *logos* to extricate itself from the chaos of *muthos*. Developing Lévi-Strauss' suggestion that lameness, stammering, and forgetfulness express blocked channels of communication, Vernant presents Oedipus as overcoming the limitations of straight walking and thinking only to fall farther when he does obtain the awesome answers he seeks to his riddles.

CENTERING STRUCTURAL ANALYSIS

To abet the continuous studies of classical mythology Vernant founded the Center for the Comparative Study of Ancient Societies within the Ecole Pratique des Hautes Etudes. During the mid-1960s Vernant began to rally some of his colleagues at the Ecole Pratique to the cause of incorporating structural analysis into classical philology and scholarship. He began working with Marcel Detienne, who had already considerable philological expertise in Greek. Vernant was intent on moving from the surface text of myths "to the structural framework that provides the overall key we can use to decipher a veritable system of thought not, at every level, immediately accessible to the habitual working of our minds."[23] The Center has become a forum for discussing a "structural framework" within traditional classical scholarship. The accessibility of the structural framework is also at issue because for Vernant as well as for Lévi-Strauss the crucial functions and meanings of myths do not reside at the surface level. Instead, the surface must be probed for indicators about where else to look. According to Vernant, two factors can facilitate that search: 1) historical distance from antiquity and 2) the comparison of Greek myths with those of other cultures. Both of these factors have been inspired by Lévi-Strauss and yet prepare a new era in the structural analysis of myths as they are allied with the contextual methods of the Gernet Center.

Vernant identifies the central contextualist problem for the study of Greek myths as the evolution of the relationship between *muthos* and *logos*. Philological study determines that "the Greek word *muthos* means formulated speech, whether it be a story, a dialogue, or the enunciation of a plan ... does not originally stand in contrast to *logoi*, a term that has a closely related semantic significance and that is concerned with the different forms of what is said."[24] However, thanks to Thucydides (431-404 B.C.), historical reporting was invented to counter the fabulous elements of myths. Aristotle (384-322 B.C.) continued to advocate *logos* as representative of a new kind of discourse used by historians and philosophers to convey truth by rules of demonstration and clarity rather than, as in myth, allegorically and indirectly. The evolution of the primacy of *logos* within Greek society is crucial to the metamorphoses of myths into the subjects of tragedies. Vernant is especially interested in the simultaneous emergence in Athens of the city, its legal system, and tragedy. Applying his theory of overlapping semantic fields, he observes that "the tragic poets use these vocabularies of law, religion, and politics, playing on the differences between semantic fields, contrasting them in order to emphasize the ambiguity of certain notions."[25] Vernant and his colleagues at the Center explore these ambiguities for commentaries on the nature of Greek society and its myths.

Besides Lévi-Strauss, Vernant has been generally inspired by two mentors: Louis Gernet and Ignace Meyerson. Some of his critics identify two Vernants in these influences—the good one listening to Gernet and the bad one following Meyerson.[26] In actuality, both figures shaped Vernant's own vision of a contextualist structural analysis. On the one hand Gernet was a historian of Greek law who gave the contextualist school insights into the evolution within Greek society of such concepts as right, morality, law, and justice through his precise definitions of the philological meanings of Greek terms. His lectures and articles[27] are cited by all the members of the Center as they seek clues for the legal contexts of myths, tragedies, and other Greek phenomena. Vernant admits that, although Gernet did not write anything on tragedy himself, his mastery of philology, law, social, political, and economic history provided the bases for generations of scholars to study Greek tragedy. Even Meyerson acknowledged the role that Gernet had in the psychological circles of Paris during his lifetime.[28]

On the other hand Meyerson, while less widely known than Gernet, guided Vernant in bringing together the methods of history and psychology. The combination of the two disciplines gives Vernant the opportunity to move between the context and the text of a myth with ease and insight. For example, his discovery of the scapegoat rituals and political ostracism becomes incisive for understanding the drives of

Oedipus, who would have self-knowledge even at the price of the realization of his fate as a "lame tyrant." The influence of both Gernet and Meyerson has become crucial in the research by all the members of the Center as they develop the implications of Vernant's model of structural analysis. Vernant and Vidal-Naquet have defined the fundamental purpose of structural analysis as "break[ing] down the mythological account so as to pick out the primary elements in it and then set[ting] these beside those to be found on other versions of the same myth or in different collections of legends."[29] One of those primary elements is the characteristic called "cunning intelligence" (*mètis*). Vernant and Detienne have collaborated on a book describing the implications of this concept for Greek culture. Cunning intelligence is conventionally considered to be the trait which Odysseus demonstrated throughout Homer's *Odyssey* (c. 700 B.C.). Vernant and Detienne have discovered the consistent valorization of cunning intelligence in the myths of Zeus, Antilochus, Hephaestus, and of course Athena, the goddess of wisdom and protectress of Odysseus. Once again, the structuralist attitude, inspired by the early attachment of Detienne for "structuralist" methods, is to go beyond the obvious in the search for a meaning residing at some level of language other than its literal sense. Their definition for cunning intelligence is worth recalling:

> it implies a complex but very coherent body of mental attitudes and intellectual behavior which combine flair, wisdom, forethought, subtlety of mind, deception, resourcefulness, vigilance, opportunism, various skills, and experience acquired over the years.[30]

Vernant and Detienne see themselves as archaeologists probing the surfaces of myths for other examples of cunning intelligence as a pervasive value in the Greek world.

Vernant's work on cunning intelligence also considers the condition of women in Greek society. His work prepares the way for feminist scholars such as Nicole Loraux to do more sophisticated inquiries into Greek womanhood. Vernant as well as Detienne and Vidal-Naquet incorporates information on Greek women in his research. While gender research is not their principal aim, their interest in such issues as Hestia as the goddess of the hearth (Vernant), the women disciples of Dionysus (Detienne), and the similar legal rights of Greek women and slaves (Vidal-Naquet) makes it easier for feminists to explore an area which has been opened for discussion. Vernant and Detienne point out that the word *mètis* comes from the goddess of that name who was swallowed by Zeus upon her pregnancy with Athena so that he could possess all of Athena's traits of wily intellectual sophistication and preclude their being used against him. The incarnation of this positive characteristic in a goddess is crucial since "certain aspects of *mètis* tend to associate it with the disloyal trick, the perfidious lie, treachery—all of which are the despised weapons of women and cowards."[31] The prejudicial association of cunning intelligence and women was part of a much larger ideology invented by Greek men about women.

Vernant argues that Hesiod's narrative of the mythical creation of the first woman, Pandora, by Zeus was used as a justification for the political situation of Greek women. Greek women were not citizens and so did not have the right to vote. Pandora was Zeus' response to Prometheus, the Titan, who challenged the Olympian gods by stealing fire for humanity and by tricking Zeus with the division of an animal's meat (for humans) and its innards for the gods. Meat, fire, and women in Hesiod's *Theogony* are thus tightly knit. Zeus has the last word:

> By creating her [woman], Zeus pulls off his master coup. He ends the game with Prometheus. The Titan can no longer respond .... The *anthropoi* [men as the single race of humanity] are forced into an ongoing confrontation and need to live with this "half" of themselves created for them with the intention of masking them what they are, *andres* [humanity divided into men and women].[32]

Vernant thus presents the mythical creation of woman as a scourge given to mankind by the gods. He might have added that both Zeus and Prometheus were using cunning intelligence well before the arrival of women, so that the Greek association of *mètis* with feminine wile was especially unfair.

Vernant's study of the goddess Hestia, patroness of the hearth and the home, reveals the static ideal of Greek society, in contrast to the politically active Greek represented by the Hermes. The static ideal was protected by Hestia in the home, where the hearth became her altar and the familial center. She represented the disfranchised lot of Greek women, whose fixed position in the home was the basis for the organization of both family and territory, as signified by the single Greek word for both concepts, *oikos*. The family and territorial rights associated with it were characterized by a division of labor, marriage, and consanguinity based on the opposition of the gods Hermes/Hestia. Vernant notes that these two deities were associated with a chthonic rather than Olympian value system that imitated the placement of the members of Greek society. The lot of women was based upon assumptions about their place in the hearth represented as a closed and static center for women by the goddess Hestia. This closed feminine space was constantly reaffirmed by moral judgments of woman's place such as that by the playwright Menander (342-289 B.C.): "a virtuous woman should stay at home, only light women appear in the streets."[33] The political situation of women in the tragedies reflects the reality of their condition in society:

> Only men can be qualified representatives of the city; women are alien to political life. That is why the members of the chorus (not to mention the actors) are always and exclusively male. Even when the chorus is supposed to represent a group of young girls or women, as is the case in a whole series of plays, those who represent it are men, suitably disguised and masked.[34]

Vernant's insights help "unmask" Oedipus from the complex
that Freud invented. However, the female masks worn by men
on the stage are only mentioned by Vernant and referred to by
his colleagues Nicole Loraux, Florence Dupont, and Suzanne
Saïd in their situations of Greek women (see chapters seven
and eight). Vernant is sensitive to the masculine domination of
a woman's identity,[35] but he does not elaborate the issue.

Vernant seeks to reveal the intersection of 1) myth, 2)
thought, and 3) society. These are the three points of a triangle
forming the geometry of Greek society. For Vernant,
geometry holds the key to understanding the "whole" of his
contextual method. Geometry entails the organization of space
and the relationships among the parameters of that space.
Vernant places structural analysis within a larger network than
the semantic structuralism of Lévi-Strauss. He includes the 1)
syntax and logic of a myth, 2) the semantic content of the
same myth, and 3) its structural context.

In order to specify this tripartite influence on tragedy,
Vernant speaks of the three historical aspects of tragedy:
social, aesthetic, and psychological. These aspects generally
conform to the 1) semantic, 2) syntactic, and 3) contextual
parameters of structural analysis and demarcate the social and
cultural environment in which the individual in ancient
Greece passed on and rejected myth by placing its story on the
stage of tragedy.

MYTH AND THE DISTRIBUTION OF SOCIAL POWER

According to Vernant, myth had an ambivalent status for
the Greeks. Because of its dual status as a fiction (stories about
the origins of the universe and humanity) and an absurdity
(divine explanations for human phenomena) myth held a
tenuous role in Greek society. As a fiction, myth incorporated
within its stories the truth of reality. In Greek truth is *aletheia.*
According to the German philosopher Martin Heidegger
(1889-1976), the literal meaning (the privative *a* and the noun
letheia) is "uncovering."[36] Vernant never cites Heidegger,[37]
probably because of Heidegger's political stigma or, more

mundanely, because of his loose way of applying self-derived etymologies to Greek terms and concepts. Nevertheless, Vernant also understands structure to be something that is uncovered. For example, his presentation of myth entails its opposition to what is not myth so that reality is the antonym that sets up myth as a fiction. By determining what was reality for the Greeks, Vernant arrives at the fiction of myth.

The struggle between *muthos* and *logos* took place in the sixth century B.C. In Ionia the pre-Socratic mathematicians Thales, Anaximander, and Anaximenes advocated a new method of thinking (*logos*) to replace creation myths. Their alternative, according to Vernant, "sought to base the order of the world on relations of symmetry, equilibrium, and equality among the various elements that made up the cosmos."[38] Thus geometry became the handmaiden of philosophy in the birth of Greek rationality. Parmenides of Miletus introduced the philosophical abstraction of Being and Knowing. Geometry and philosophy allowed no place for *muthos*.

Vernant notes three implications from the cosmologies associated with creation myths: 1) the universe is a hierarchy of power, and gods are distinguished in function, value, and rank; 2) the world emerges in dramatic fashion with gods; and 3) the power of the gods is monarchical over humans. In the Oedipus myth, for example, the deities Pelops and Hera (1) lay curses on the family of Laius for the rape of Chrysippus (2). Oedipus was being punished for his father's crime by the hierarchically empowered gods (3).

The new geometric order (*isonomia*) of equilibrium, order, and symmetry provided the parameters for Sophocles' Oedipus to become subject to the human drama with the application of the scapegoat ritual, political ostracism, and finally suicide. Sophocles adds rational human order to provide a transition for the Oedipus myth as part of a new image of the world. The sense of justice (*dike*) as divine will is no longer acceptable to the Greeks, who are now intent upon setting up a democratic government in which human reason enables people to govern themselves. Once again, the shift from myth to tragedy reflects the shift from monarchy to democracy with consequent shifts in power and responsibility for action from gods to humanity.

Hesiod, together with Homer, provides Vernant with the source for the fictional distribution of power in Greek myth. In *Works and Days* Hesiod presents the "myth of the races," whereby time proceeds though five stages, four metal deteriorating from the gold to the iron ages and one heroic age. Vernant interprets Hesiod's time as cyclical rather than linear because "it is a time which consists not so much of a succession of moments, but rather of a stratification of layers, where the different ages are superimposed upon the other."[39] This portrayal has been attacked by scholars as being a violation of Hesiod's diachronic order.[40] Vernant's response is that, rather than opposing structure to chronology, he is showing their compatibility. Temporality can take a form other than that of mere linear sequence. The rhythm of the past is better understood if the myth of the races is seen as a series of genealogies rather than as a simple chronology.

Vernant also stresses that the necessary counterpart to recollecting the past, as myths do, is to forget the present. In this way *muthos* becomes identified as fictive and cyclical; and the new rationality, by focusing on the eternally present, gets associated with linear reality.

Myths retain the memory of what would otherwise be forgotten. The example of cunning intelligence, as distributed among the deities of Mt. Olympus, appears somewhat gratuitous at first glance. However, Vernant observes that "the distribution of power among the various figures in the pantheon inevitably entails some degree of sharing out this form of intelligence."[41] This "sharing out"—for example, in Homer's association of the goddess Athena with Odysseus—explains why cunning intelligence cannot be simply called forth by anyone at any time, as the proponents of *logos* expected of other kinds of human reasoning.

The fictionalized accounts of *muthos* provide places for various kinds of human conduct. These places are imaginary, divine, or etiological locations which specify human behavior within a certain context. Vernant especially presents Greek myth as characterized by an order that geometry and philosophy would later develop into rules and precepts. Even the gods represent an order to be emulated by the human organization of power:

> Every god is defined by the network of relations which links him [sic] with and opposes him [sic] to the other deities included within a particular pantheon; and similarly, a single detail in a myth is only significant by virtue of its place within the ordered system in which the myth itself belongs.[42]

This comment epitomizes the contextualist argument preferring a specifically Greek set of links to a universal view of linkage. Vernant observes a statue by the sculptor Phidias (b. 490 B.C.) in which twelve Greek gods are paired beneath Zeus on Mount Olympus. The pairing of Hestia and Hermes as divine counterparts to the human division of labor by gender reflects the Greek attitude toward "the ordered system." Hestia in fact represents the "dispersion of centralization"[43] away from the monarchical system of Zeus and Hermes and toward the human arena, where another order, the city and its democratic rule according to the principles of *logos*, was being formed.

The contextualist presentation of the struggle of myth with the rising values of the Greek city-state incorporates the strengths of three major theories of myth while also adding another dimension. As noted, Vernant identifies these theories as the symbolic, the functionalist, and the structuralist.

The symbolic theory, advanced by the German philosopher Ernst Cassirer (1874-1945) and the French philosopher Paul Ricoeur (b. 1913), views the symbols in myths as expressions of abstract ideas. Symbols in myths are assumed to express abstract ideas and the universal powers of human reason underlying them. In taking the riddle of Oedipus' identity as a symbol of ambivalence in Greek culture, Vernant follows the symbolists.

The functionalist theory of myth was developed by the Polish anthropologist Bronislaw Malinowski (1884-1942). Functionalists stipulate that each constituent element of a cultural system is explained by its role within that system.

Myths play a certain role integrally linked with varying aspects of the cultures in which they are found. The influence of functionalism on Vernant is evident in his linkage of the myth of Oedipus to various Greek rituals and, more generally, to fifth century Greek culture. Both the symbolic and the functionalist theories help Vernant to modify the third major contemporary theory of myth: Lévi-Strauss' structuralism. Vernant acknowledges that Lévi-Strauss introduced new questions for myth analysis. Lévi-Strauss proposes the possibility of deciphering a myth independent of the civilization that produced it. Vernant seeks not to reject structuralism but to combine it with symbolism and especially functionalism.

The contextualist school uses philology to introduce a diachronic axis into myth analysis. Philology provides insight into the significance of written myths by tracing the evolution of terms. The word "Oedipus" as an ambivalent adaptation of the Greek words for "I know" and "swollen foot" places the character's riddle at the center of his own literal mind-body problem based originally on his name. Philology is a historical discipline privileging past meanings as insights into the functioning of language. Myth is thus a palimpsest, a text on which several previous versions are inscribed imperfectly so that words from previous adaptations are still visible. Vernant's task is to separate these versions and to comment upon which period each represents so that remembering, seeing, and knowing become interchangeable terms for the modern reader of myth. In 1966 Vernant presented his contextualist theory to a seminar on structuralism at Johns Hopkins University. We recall Derrida's comment about his disappointment with Vernant's "realistic reading"[44] of *Oedipus Rex*. That "realistic reading," however, distinguishes Vernant's structural analysis from Lévi-Strauss' structuralism and provides the setting for appreciating the fiction of myth.

THE ABSURDITY OF MYTH

By opposition to what is rational, myth also expresses, according to Vernant, a distinctively Greek penchant for the absurd. The absurd is that which is ridiculously unreasonable to the modern reader such as the supposition that, in a happier time, men dined with the gods. Vernant seeks to explain such absurdities by giving insights into the reality of the Greek world. This reality was supported by myths that, by analogy, reaffirmed the absurdities of the Hellenic world in a state of flux as the city, democracy, and tragedy were simultaneously evolving. Likewise the discursive rationality of philosophy and the analytical spirit of geometry were combining to analyze a world which had formerly been represented by myths of Olympian deeds. The pantheon passed on by Greek myths reflects "a symbolic language with its own intellectual ends."[45] The Olympian pantheon displays what Vernant calls a "network of relations" not only among the deities themselves but often in collaboration with humanity. For example, Athena is both the goddess of wisdom and the patroness of Odysseus who becomes renowned for his cunning intelligence. The classificatory system of the myths is beneficial to order both within a divine scheme and within human affairs. In the Oedipus myth the divine curses of Pelops and Hera are communicated through oracles. At Delphi, Oedipus consults an oracle to learn of his fate to kill his father and sleep with his mother. This information spurs his departure from Corinth, where he assumes his parents, Polybus and Merope, reside, and his journey to Thebes, where his fate will be realized. For Vernant, human memory is "comparable to the journey which is mimed out in certain consultations of oracle: the descent of a living person into the underworld for the purpose of finding out—and seeing—what he wants to know."[46] The fate of humanity is thus intertwined with the classificatory schemes of the gods, who control human access to the orderly schemes of fate.

Vernant identifies the concepts that underlie this description of fate within myths. He is especially intrigued by the concepts of space, time, and number as they are wrapped in the folds of myth. Since humanity and divinity occupy distinct races, the differences and similarities in their lots are especially informative about the nature of humanity. Hermes and Hestia are paired as part of the global social scheme to describe the active and passive lots of men and women in Greek society. The contest between Zeus and Prometheus explains the differentiation of mankind (*anthropoi*) into an androgynous being (*andres*) divided by two genders—an explanation that must, of course, be offered as the justification by a male-dominated society for the loss of a once single-gendered race that sat down to dine with the gods.

The dual-value system is part of a much more universal trait of Greek myth: "thus myth brings into operation a form of logic which we may describe, in contrast to the logic of the philosophers, as a logic of the ambiguous, the equivocal, a logic of polarity."[47] Equivocation lies at the heart of the absurdities found in Greek myths.

The absurdities of Greek myths return us to Derrida's disappointment about the realism of Vernant's *Oedipus Rex*. Derrida's disappointment should be understood to signify that Vernant does not fit the mold of expectations about French structuralism in the wake of Lévi-Strauss. Vernant takes the semantic work of Lévi-Strauss a step further by integrating the intellectual framework produced by the grids of structural analysis into the sociohistorical context of the myth. The myths about the noble death of a Greek warrior attract Vernant's "realism." Sparta advocated the various absurdities about glorifying the death of a warrior into a matter of prestige for the individual and for the glory of the city-state. Even Athens cultivated such a view of the noble death on a more restricted scale, as evidenced by the funeral orations investigated by Vernant's colleague Nicole Loraux. Nevertheless, it is Vernant who first analyzes the Greek mythical presentation of death.

First of all, Vernant reminds us that "when women did not yet exist—before Pandora was created—death did not exist for men either."[48] For the Greeks, women and death are afflictions to males brought on by the gods. The myth of the noble death allowed men to transcend both afflictions. A male warrior could attain a privileged situation with the gods, thereby recalling that special time when men and gods had dined together. Death was thus not an affliction but a noble act. The warrior status and a noble death were denied women. In these two conditions men could act as if Pandora had never come. Of course, the special status given to the noble death fostered an altruism and an idealism that helped to sustain the military career and to defend the city-state from its enemies.

In this twilight zone of reality men often ceased to be part of the human race also. Vernant recalls the passages from the *Odyssey* where, in their desperation to obtain food, Odysseus' shipmates from the domain of the sun-god resort to cannibalism. As Vernant concludes, in both cases these men cease to be human beings,[49] on the one hand by not respecting the boundaries between men and gods and on the other hand by not respecting the boundaries between men and animals. This inhumanity of the warrior especially returns the absurdity of this myth to reality when the historians begin recording the social outrage over the many warriors whose bodies were left to rot on the field of battle because they had died in a losing cause. The abandoned cadaver signifies the inverse of the mythic noble death, the grounding of that absurdity in the reality of the horrors of war for the male who thinks that war gives him a privileged perspective.[50] Vernant's insistence upon portraying the "network of relations" both internal and external to myths entails such a reality, as "disappointing" or "unstructuralist" as it may appear to some. Nevertheless, his leadership in this variety of structural analysis has inspired others. One of these, Marcel Detienne, is the subject of the next chapter.

NOTES

1. Claude Lévi-Strauss with Didier Eribon, *De Près et de loin* (Paris: Odile Jacob, 1988), p. 105.

2. See chapters two through six of my *French Structuralism* (Boston: G. K. Hall and Co., 1990) for more elaborate presentations of these writers as the principal ideologists for this intellectual circle.

3. Jean-Pierre Vernant, *Myth and Thought among the Greeks*, tr. not given (London: Routledge & Kegan Paul, 1983), p. 220.

4. Jean-Pierre Vernant, "Greek Tragedy: Problems of Interpretation," in *The Structuralist Controversy: The Languages of Criticism and the Sciences of Man*, eds. Richard Macksey and Eugenio Donato (Baltimore: Johns Hopkins University Press, 1972), p. 273.

5. Jean-Pierre Vernant, *Myth and Society in Ancient Greece*, tr. Janet Lloyd (New York: Zone Books, 1988), p. 259.

6. Vernant, "Greek Tragedy," p. 289.

7. Jean-Pierre Vernant, "The Myth of Prometheus in Hesiod," in *Myth, Religion & Society*, ed. R. L. Gordon (Cambridge: Cambridge University Press, 1981), p. 50.

8. Jean-Pierre Vernant, "The Reason of Myth," in his *Myth and Society in Ancient Greece*, tr. Janet Lloyd (New York: Zone Books, 1988), pp. 203-79.

9. *Ibid.*, p. 225.

10. *Ibid.*, p. 205.

11. *Ibid.*, p. 215.

12. Vernant, "Intimations of the Will in Greek Tragedy," in Vernant and Pierre Vidal-Naquet, *Myth and Tragedy in Ancient Greece*, tr. Janet Lloyd (Sussex: Harvester Press, 1981), p. 71.

13. Vernant, "Aeschylus, the Past and the Present," in *Myth and Society*, p. 253.

14. Vernant, "The Lame Tyrant," in *Myth and Society*, p. 230.

15. *Ibid.*, p. 207.

16. The three essays containing Vernant's reading of the Oedipus myth are found in *Myth and Tragedy in Ancient Greece* and are entitled: "Oedipus Without the Complex" (pp. 85-112), "Ambiguity and Reversal" (pp. 113-40), and "The Lame Tyrant" (pp. 207-36).

17. See chapter nine of my *French Structuralism* for a more elaborate presentation of Girard as a French structuralist. For a discussion of the importance of sacrifice and the scapegoat, see René Girard, *The Violence and the Sacred*, tr. Patrick Gregory (Baltimore: Johns Hopkins University Press, 1977), and *The Scapegoat*, tr. Yvonne Freccero (Baltimore: Johns Hopkins University Press, 1986).

18. Ignace Meyerson did not publish much on "historical psychology." See his *Les Fonctions psychologiques et les oeuvres* (Paris: J. Vrin, 1948) and Zevedei Barbu's *Problems of Historical Psychology* (London: Routledge & Kegan Paul, 1960).

19. Vernant, "Imitations of the Will in Greek Tragedy," in *Myth and Tragedy*, p. 64.

20. Vernant, "Greek Tragedy," p. 293.

21. Jean-Pierre Vernant, "Ambiguity and Reversal: On the Enigmatic Structure of *Oedipus Rex*," *New Literary History*, IX (1977-78), p. 480.

22. Vernant, "Greek Tragedy," p. 291.

23. Vernant, " The Reason of Myth," p. 225.

24. *Ibid.*, pp. 203-4.

25. Vernant, "Greek Tragedy," p. 275.

26. Vincenzo Di Benedetto and Alessandro Lami, *Filologia e marxismo—Contra le mistificazioni* (Naples: Liguori, 1981), pp. 107-14.

27. A bibliography of Gernet's work is appended to *Hommage à Louis Gernet* (Paris: Presses Universitaires de France, 1966), pp. 43-48.

28. Ignace Meyerson, "L'Oeuvre psychologique de Louis Gernet," in *Hommage à Louis Gernet*, pp. 38-42.

29. Vernant and Vidal-Naquet, p. 8.

30. Marcel Detienne and Jean-Pierre Vernant, *Cunning Intelligence in Greek Culture and Society*, tr. Janet Lloyd (Atlantic Highlands, N.J.: Harvester Press, 1978), p. 3.

31. *Ibid.*, p. 13.

32. Vernant, in his and Marcel Detienne's *The Cuisine of Sacrifice among the Greeks*, tr. Paula Wissing (Chicago: University of Chicago Press, 1989), p. 62.

33. Cited by Vernant in his *Myth and Thought among the Greeks*, p. 164, n. 27.

34. Vernant, "The Historical Moment of Tragedy in Greece: Some of the Social and Psychological Conditions," in *Myth and Tragedy*, p. 23, n. 2.

35. For example, Vernant notes that "in a masculine society such as that of Greece the woman is normally regarded from the man's point of view" (*Myth and Thought*, pp. 138-9).

36. Martin Heidegger, *Being and Time*, trs. John Macquarrie and Edward Robinson (New York: Harper & Row, 1962), pp. 262ff.

37. Robert Pogue Harrison ("The Ambiguities of Philology," *Diacritics*, XVI, 2 [Summer 1986], p. 15) remarks that Marcel Detienne similarly avoids Heidegger's obvious precedent as part of the Gernet School's position as a bastion of "liberal philology" and representative of its "hostility toward philosophers." In an interview with me on July 7, 1989, Vidal-Naquet, as Director of the School, pointed out that Vernant was trained as a philosopher and that his example is respected by all its members. Nevertheless, Heidegger is more universally respected as a philosopher than as a philologist. Philology is an abiding concern of many of the School's members: Gernet, Detienne, Loraux, Vidal-Naquet, and even Vernant himself.

38. Jean-Pierre Vernant, *The Origins of Greek Thought*, tr. not given (Ithaca: Cornell University Press, 1982), p. 11.

39. Vernant, *Myth and Thought among the Greeks*, p. 121.

40. J. Delfradas, "Le Mythe hésiodique des races," *L'Information littéraire*, IV (1965), pp. 152-56.

41. Vernant in *Cunning Intelligence*, p. 279.

42. Vernant, Introduction to Marcel Detienne, *The Gardens of Adonis*, tr. Janet Lloyd (Sussex: Harvester Press, 1977), p. iii.

43. Thomas di Piero, "A Myth is as Good as a Smile," *Diacritics*, XVI, 2 (Summer 1986), p. 25.

44. Jacques Derrida, Discussion, in *The Structuralist Controversy*, p. 294.

45. Vernant, *Myth and Society*, p. 10.

46. Vernant, *Myth and Thought among the Greeks*, p. 80.

47. Vernant, *Myth and Society*, p. 239.

48. Jean-Pierre Vernant, "Feminine Figures of Death in Greece," tr. Anne Doueihi, *Diacritics*, XVI, 2 (Summer 1986), p. 56.

49. Jean-Pierre Vernant, "Manger au pays du Soleil," in *Culture science et développement: mélanges et l'honneur de Charles Morazé*, ed. not given (Toulouse: Privat, 1979), p. 61.

50. My translation of Jean-Pierre Vernant, "La Belle Mort et le cadavre outragé," in *La Mort, les morts dans les sociétés anciennes*, eds. Vernant and Gherardo Gnoli (Cambridge: Cambridge University Press, 1982), p. 69.

Chapter Five

DETIENNE: THE EMPIRICAL CATEGORIES OF MYTH

Of all the members of the Gernet School, Marcel Detienne
has been the one most involved in distinguishing the *structural
analysis* of the contextualists from the structuralism of Lévi-
Strauss. Presently the Director of Studies and Chair of the
History of Greek Religions at the Ecole des Hautes Etudes,
Detienne has used his philological training to bring together
history and structural analysis. His method has evolved from
a close application of the cognitive categories of structuralism
to an application to written myths of the Asdiwal
"ethnographic context" by Lévi-Strauss. As he puts it in his
Dionysus Slain:

> To discover the complete horizon of a society's
> symbolic values, it is also necessary to map out its
> transgressions, interrogate its deviants, discern
> phenomena of rejection and refusal, and circumscribe
> the silent myths that unlock upon underlying
> knowledge and the implicit.[1]

The "silent myths" have been at the center of Detienne's
research. Using his philological acumen to trace the evolution
of crucial Greek concepts such as *daîmon* (the way gods speak
through human intuition), *mètis* (cunning intelligence), and
myrrh (the spice), he begins his self-described
"archaeological"[2] dig, his quest for "underlying knowledge and
the implicit," into new empirical categories for myths. The
categories are initially the concepts themselves. Detienne
inserts them as wedges into much broader problems addressed

by Greek myths: the silent myths about the roles of women
and the nature of blood sacrifice.

After having experimented with comparative cognitive
categories like zoological, dietary, and astronomical codes for
plants in his *The Gardens of Adonis* (1977), Detienne has
become convinced of the more expansive vision offered by the
ethnographic context for philology. Prior to his acquaintance
with the Asdiwal model, Detienne followed the more typical
Lévi-Strauss: history did not play a significant role in the
decisions about which were pertinent analytical categories.
Etymological studies of terms such as *daîmon* and *mètis* did
give him insights into possible epistemological categories, but
there were no consistent or thorough methodological ties
between the historical context and the formation of those
categories.

The Asdiwal model showed that the historical context and
the structuralist paradigm could be united. Detienne
recognized that the written myth in a literate culture provided
more information upon which to base the ethnographic
method. The vertical grid of cognitive categories could be
more solidly based on a firm knowledge of its horizontal
footing. Detienne expresses his conviction that a structural
method could be more convincingly exemplified in the Greek
culture, about which so much is known: "The semantics of
myth is richer for being discovered through syntax."[3] The
semantic structuralism of Lévi-Strauss can thus be enhanced
by the syntactic context that Detienne's philology brings to the
analysis of myths. Rather than the historical psychology of
Vernant, with its promotion of the service of history and the
structural method to a philosophical attitude about the values
of the Greeks, Detienne promises a diligent understanding of
the evolution of the Greek mind by the subordination of the
structural method to that insight. To the degree that Detienne
clings to his identity as a philologist, history is never very far
from his kind of structural analysis.

Detienne's style emanates from his need to see the world
through the eyes of the Greeks. Employing a variation of the
Socratic method, Detienne often asks questions in his writings
to engender discussion within his own text. Detienne's

questioning, however, does not receive direct answers. Instead, he uses questions rhetorically to push the horizons of his discussion. This technique reinforces Vernant's theory about the inherently ambivalent nature of myths—there being no single reading for most myths. Detienne's style reflects that of the myth or the matter he is reviewing. In this way Detienne is similar to Plato who imitates the style of his teacher, Socrates, to convey his own doctrines in a subtle orientation of the dialogues. As some may ask whether Socrates or Plato is sometimes speaking, so with Detienne some ask whether the empirical categories are those of the myth or of the analyst.

Nevertheless, Detienne distinguishes himself from Lévi-Strauss, of whom the same is asked, by the kinds of myths that he studies. As opposed to the oral traditions that interest Lévi-Strauss, Detienne focuses on the written myths of the Greeks. The written myths bring different sets of problems because of their documentary nature and the literate audience to whom they were addressed. The written myths can more easily be repeated in the same way because they are inscribed. Their readers can return to a story if interrupted or merely to appreciate it once again. And they see the same details recounted. As Robert Segal points out, Detienne believes that "once written down, they [myths] become fixed, hence distant, hence in need of explication."[4]

The written myths become mythology, which has two divergent meanings for Detienne:[5] 1) the myths or stories themselves, and 2) a discourse about myths. This distinction between myth and mythology enables Detienne to separate the commentators from the stories themselves. While he points to the universal belief that "no people exists whose history does not begin with fables or mythology,"[6] that very history is an elaboration or discourse about the significance of the fables. The Greeks themselves separated real (or credible) history (*logos*) from the fantastic stories of *muthos*. Detienne invokes Phaedrus asking Socrates: "Do you believe that this talk about myths is true?" Although the question was not succinctly answered by Socrates, Detienne offers a modern rejoinder in the explorations of the connections between the stories and the discourse about them. These connections offer what he calls

"the semantic crossroads of two discourses,"[7] the first being
a specific myth and the second being its setting within Greek
culture. He especially enjoys elaborating the crossroads of
logos and *muthos* of science and religion. Let us see how
Detienne might read the Oedipus myth.

A DIONYSIAC READING OF OEDIPUS

Detienne has not yet published a reading of Oedipus. In
his essay "The Greeks aren't like the others" (in *Dionysus
Slain*), he criticizes Lévi-Strauss' reading of Oedipus as "the
choice of a huckster."[8] Lévi-Strauss is a peddler who
borrowed his matrix from the sociology of Marie Delcourt.
Detienne would have preferred a more thorough presentation
by Lévi-Strauss of the ethnographical context, as Lévi-Strauss
did later.

I offer here what I take to be a Detienne-like reading of
the Oedipus myth based on his research into the Dionysiac
cults. Detienne assumes that Lévi-Strauss has changed forever
the ways classicists situate mythology by directing the focus
away from the narrative of the myth to the structure—1)
myths are now reduced to synopses of their narration rather
than distinguished according to variants; synopses replace the
actual stories of myths; 2) the condition of myths as narratives
affects the very texture of myths; the conditions ("the texture")
of narrating a myth explain the rules by which a myth is
composed; 3) the mythical narrative is a component of the
composition rules for choral lyric and tragedy; the rules
usually refer to aspects beyond the narrated story or its
variants (choral lyric and dramatic event in the case of Greek
tragedy). Detienne himself returns to the discarded narrative
and its historical context and adapts the structuralist approach
to what he calls "an alternative total history."[9]

Lévi-Strauss views myth as representative of the human
spirit. Vernant views myth as the expression of the psychology
of a particular culture. By contrast to both, Detienne is
concerned with the subversive effect of myth on a historical
situation. The analyst must be well informed about the "total"

cultural situation of a myth to be able to identify how that myth modifies the culture in which it appears. For Greek tragedy, this information is especially significant since the chorus provides an alternative voice to those of the characters. Detienne situates the problem of mythology in tragedy thus: "the ancient values that mythology brings to bear are confronted with those that the city is busy constructing and whose antagonistic spokesman is embodied in the chorus."[10] Myth is to culture as the chorus in tragedy is to the characters (or hero) as the countryside is to the city, and as *muthos* is to *logos*.

One of the subversive groups set against the formation of the city-state was the Dionysiac cult—formed around Bacchus, the god of wines, and his alter ego, Dionysus, the god of revelry, madness, and violent human defilement. Detienne points out that the Dionysiac religion questioned the social relevance of the incest taboo, which occupied Oedipus. This cult reenacted the death of Dionysus, who was literally dismembered and eaten by the Titans, the predecessors of humans. Maenads, mythical women dedicated to the cult of Dionysus, celebrated his death through orgiastic dances in which other humans or animals were dismembered and whose flesh was eaten raw (omophagia). According to the *Bacchae* of Euripides (485-406 B.C.), women of Thebes were reputed to have joined in the frenzy of the Maenads. The dances were part of the religious tribute to the foot or the leg as the key part of the Dionysiac body. Detienne recalls that "the bacchic step, the quick forward thrust of the [right] foot, was taught to choruses of satyrs in Athens around 500 B.C. by the dancing master Pratinas ...."[11] The inebriated state of those partaking in wine festivals lent itself to the identification of the stumble and the leap with the more sedate, divine alter ego of Bacchus. The Dionysiac cult's obsession with the foot provides insights into the significance of Oedipus' limp for the Greek audience. His limping serves as a counterpoint to his conscious search for self-identity and legitimacy, a search that was poignant for the Greeks in their politics of the city-state.

The Dionysiac practices isolated by Detienne provide a backdrop to Oedipus the cripple haunted by his drive for self-knowledge and the ultimate "crimes" of patricide, incest, and suicide. Vernant's analysis of the crippled condition of Oedipus is enriched by Detienne's observation that in *Antigone* the god Dionysus is invoked by reference to his divine foot.[12] Oedipus also had the "unsteady foot" of Dionysus as he stumbled along trying to solve the question of his legitimate identity. His violent acts, crimes according to the rules of Greek society, were the result of his frenzy to know who he was. The reasonable order of the city, representing the new values of *logos* and the goal of self-knowledge, was represented in its rulers, the class to which Oedipus was born and to which he also acceded in Thebes. His swollen foot signifies the subversion of that order by such cults as that of the Dionysiacs, who promoted the rituals and sacrifices of *muthos*. Oedipus the cripple could not rule directly. His abandonment at birth, when he was crippled, meant his ostracism from the ruling class. Nor could Oedipus pursue his self-knowledge as steadily as the advocates of the city thought natural for humanity. He consulted the oracle to begin the course of his enlightenment. Oedipus was not the erect human but the frenzied dancer who stumbled, as if inebriated by the "reasonable" pursuit of self-knowledge, and acted in violation of the laws of the city to which he had never belonged anyway.

Appropriately, Detienne notes that, at the Bacchic wine festivals, "for the amusement of those who remained seated on the ground, the contestants were obliged to leap ... to test their already compromised equilibrium."[13] Similarly, the audience of the Greek tragedies of Oedipus was on the ground watching Oedipus stumble and leap toward the frenzied destruction of himself and his family, which was supposed to be the nucleus for the city's new political order. The Dionysiacs could enjoy the ultimate acts of Oedipus, not so much as crimes but as signs of the blood sacrifice necessitated by the redistribution of political power in the rising city. The acts of Oedipus were thus ritual reenactments of the Titans' slaying of Dionysus, who had been born out of Zeus' very thigh. Dionysus was sacrificed to the barbarism of the Titans, who challenged the rule by Zeus and the Olympians. Similarly, Oedipus was a martyr to the need for identity and legitimacy within the Greek city.

In Detienne, myth is connected to politics by offering witness to the turmoil of a particular moment in history. The Dionysiac myths and rituals both clarify the tragic variant of the Oedipus myth and offer a commentary on the historical evolution of the city-state within the struggle between *logos* and *muthos*. This reading provides a mutual commentary between the context and the text so that each is an expansion upon the other.

For the Lévi-Strauss of even Asdiwal, the ethnographic context is merely the point of departure for establishing semantic fields within myths and is not enriched by the myth. These "semantic fields" are discussions of meaning that all peoples share. For Vernant and for initially for Detienne as well, the setting of the myth likewise provides the philosophical, rather than the semantic characteristics of the human spirit, parameters for the discussion of the social function of the myth within its specific historical setting. For Detienne, who goes beyond Vernant, the ethnographic context establishes a dialogue between the myth and its originating culture, especially one that questions and subverts the culture.

THE GREEKS AREN'T LIKE THE OTHERS

Written myths are different from oral myths. Written myths provide documents which can be verified by differing generations of readers. These documents require skilled readers whose skills affect how it is they appreciate the myths. This is the argument that Vernant and Detienne make for the contextualist school of structural analysis. Detienne pursues the written nature of these myths with studies that are a combination of philology and history.[14] Yet he recognizes that "the failure of a purely philological and historical approach to account for it [the mythical situation] satisfactorily ... justifies a structural analysis."[15] Structural analysis adds cross-cultural cognitive categories and epistemological situations because many myths were originally passed on orally and subsequently written. The question is how do readers know and assimilate myths differently if they read them rather than hear them. The Gernet School focuses on the Greeks to reply that the written history and scholarship on this culture affects how the myths are passed on from generation to generation, in other words as part of a homogeneous vision being communicated by a writer. Detienne's analysis of the myth of "honeyed Orpheus" provides an example. Originally an oral myth, the story of Orpheus and Eurydice takes a strange twist with the Aristaeus myth added by Virgil. The bee-keeper Aristaeus loses his bees because he drives Eurydice to the underworld. Through Detienne's observation of bees and the written association of scrupulous purity, chastity, and a vegetarian diet given to them by the Greeks, he discovers the key to the relationship among Aristaeus, the bee-keeper; Eurydice, the inventor of honey; and Orpheus. In written documents, the bee is the Greek symbol for the domestic virtues of the Greek married woman:

> Faithful to her husband and the mother of legitimate children, she watches over the private area of the house, taking care of the couple's possessions, always reticent and modest, so adding to the functions of a wife those of a housekeeper, never greedy or fond of drink or inclined to doze, who firmly rejects the romantic chatter that women in general enjoy.[16]

This "silent myth" of the bee (*melissa*) also entails other myths and stereotypes about women to be considered later in this chapter.

Detienne's ethnographic context elaborates sociological, cosmological, economic, geographical, and historical factors. His "alternative total history" is a combination of philology, and structure, as well as history, into a grid that has a vertical axis with levels of meaning intersecting with a horizontal axis on which myths and their historical settings are correlated. This grid is a variation of the semantic models built by Lévi-Strauss and Jakobson. Detienne is indebted to Lévi-Strauss for the ethnographic context, even though Lévi-Strauss himself used it only in the case of the Asdiwal myth. Acknowledging that "Lévi-Strauss is the one who has taught mythologists that in order to understand the signification of a plant or an animal, it is necessary to determine each time precisely which role each culture attributes to that plant or animal within a classification system,"[17] Detienne adapts the ethnographic context to written myths and applies the dynamic readings, theorized by Barthes to demonstrate the polyvalent signification of myths, to enrich both the context itself and the myth.

The ethnographic context is especially well suited for the written myths of Greek culture. After all, the word "ethnography" literally means "anthropological writing." Hence the context for this writing entails detailed studies that enable better understanding of the "semantic horizons" of the written words of the myths. In addition, Detienne incorporates symbols from Lévi-Strauss' *Mythologiques*, as if he needs the master's presence to give anthropological confirmation of his method.

But Detienne does break away from a slavish imitation of Lévi-Strauss' analysis of Asdiwal. As Detienne applies the ethnographic context to the Greek world, he is intent upon establishing the congruity of this method with the Greeks' understanding of themselves: "... the structural analysis from the outside turns out to be in agreement with the analysis which the Greeks who were contemporary with these myths elaborated from within."[18] This congruency certainly does not interest Lévi-Strauss. For Detienne, it becomes an essential criterion for his dialogue between myth and its context, especially as the myth leads to the subversion of that context.

As a "faithful Lévi-Straussian"[19] in *The Gardens of Adonis* and *Dionysus Slain*, Detienne offers considerable information about the Greek conceptions of plant and animal life. In *The Gardens of Adonis* he explains the Greek association of sexuality with various spices found in the culture. Beginning with myrrh, a spice named after the mother of Adonis and also used to produce perfumes as promoters of women's seductive power over men, he catalogues a whole range of dietary items culminating in the lettuce which the Pythagoreans, defenders of marriage, recommended in the summer as an anti-aphrodisiac. These dietary laws also involve specific attitudes toward eating animal flesh. Blood sacrifice and omophagia maintained humanity's intermediate position between divinities and beasts. Finding examples of these botanical and dietary codes in the myths of the Greeks, he observes that "the whole politico-religious system sustains [humanity's position] through the daily practice of the alimentary blood sacrifice."[20]

Commenting on Detienne's work on spices, Vernant presents the impact of Detienne's research as the elaboration of Greek culture's manifestation of how the Greeks understood themselves: "Seen as a whole, this system appears to have a fundamental social significance: it expresses how a group of people in particular historical circumstances sees itself, how it defines its condition of life and its relationship to nature and the supernatural."[21] While Detienne shows the system or code within the dietary practices of the Greeks and thus part of the codes of meaning used by the Greeks, Vernant is more philosophical in applying his own vision for social interaction with myths to explain Detienne's categories as exemplifying "a network of relations," crucial to the Gernet Center's ideology of the mythic context.

Detienne discovers that the frustrated sexuality of the mythical figure Myrrha symbolizes the ambivalent attitude of Greeks toward the spice myrrh. Myrrha scorns all the men who can possibly marry her and is passionately in love with the only person who cannot marry her: Cinyrus, her father. She is the mother of Adonis by her father and thus incarnates both erotic love and a menace to legitimate marriage. Her son carries on her role: he never marries or fathers any children. Likewise the spice named after her has an ambivalent social role. Positively, it is a perfume that induces erotic relations. Negatively, it is an ingredient in loaves, part of the human diet that separates humanity from gods and beasts. The apparently confusing attitude toward myrrh as a perfume and a spice is thus organized into a symmetrical structure.

A GRAMMAR OF A WAY OF THINKING

Detienne's collaboration with the Gernet Center eventually led him to to reexamine the claim of Lévi-Strauss that myth is so uniform universally as to be recognizable as myth by any culture. The Gernet School stresses the distinctiveness of every myth or mythology because of the distinctiveness of its context. Detienne comes to see not only that Greek myth is distinctive because its context is but language expresses that distinctiveness. As Vernant says:

> Language, in whose framework myth is constituted and formulated, overflows the domain of mythical activity; it expresses the totality of the social experience; it is all at once the instrument, the vehicle, and the manifestation of a global culture.[22]

Detienne consequently sees that his "first, and essential, task is to construct the grammar of the [Greek] way of thinking expressed in the myths."[23]

Detienne's essay "Rethinking Mythology" and book *The Creation of Mythology* contain reflections upon the historical distancing of myths and mythology, just as words and grammar are linked by the functioning of words in a system. Three pejorative uses of the word "myth" led to the creation of mythology. First, the word "myth" was introduced by Xenophanes of Colophon in 530 B.C. to condemn the stories of the gods as in reality either pure fiction or else stories about humans rather than gods. Second, in 524-522 B.C. Anacreon of Samos called people who held seditious opinions *mythietai*. Third, in the fifth century the lyric poet Pindar and the historians Herodotus and Thucydides identified themselves as "logographs" (literally, writers of reasoned discourse) and portrayed the stories of gods as unbelievable, illusory, and stupid. With Thucydides the crack in the continuous belief in myths became a breach: the reliance of history upon written documents provided a distance from the mouth-to-ear communication characteristic of the age of *muthos*. Prior to Thucydides, the Greeks had utilized exegesis to provide the commentary that myths made upon culture. "Exegesis" is the internal commentary that is made upon oneself. "Interpretation" is made from the outside by those able to stand outside a culture. "Mythology" was thus born as a vehicle for the interpretation of those stories known as myths.

According to Detienne, the commentary offered by written mythology pursues the production of meaning in myth from three different perspectives. Lévi-Strauss exemplifies the "tautegoric" approach, in which meaning is derived within mythology itself. Another approach is to go through mythology in search of an ineffable meaning beyond rational discourse, as Paul Ricoeur is wont to do. Third, there is the pursuit of meaning from outside myths in attempts to recover their historical significance, which is typically hidden. Here the Gernet Center is making its mark.

Detienne is in the forefront in using myths as keys to unlock cultural insights into the Greek world. Myths become allegories because the narratives teach lessons derived from the Greek sensibility. Three examples will suffice: the myths of Mètis, Prometheus, and the subversive cults.

Mètis, the incarnation of cunning intelligence, represents the nature of survival to those Greeks who realize that struggle is a condition of life. Detienne and Vernant trace the value of cunning intelligence in Greek culture. The myth itself is instructive since Mètis, as the first wife of Zeus and the mother of Athena, the Goddess of Wisdom, was swallowed by Zeus immediately after the birth of Athena. According to Detienne, the effect for Zeus exemplifies strategic planning for the hierarchical structure of the universe: "Not a single trick can be plotted in the universe without first passing through his mind. There can no longer be any risk to threaten the duration of the power of the sovereign god."[24] Not only do the other deities participate in this form of intelligence in order to maintain the balance of power within the Olympic pantheon, but humanity, in its intermediate position between divinity and bestiality, imitates this balance of power with the use of guile gleaned from animal life also. The fishing net, the traps, and the power of the circle are all inspired by the cunning techniques used by the octopus, the fox, and feline hunters. Humanity expands its use of wily techniques into the areas of medicine, navigation, and weaving. These techniques are epitomized in the Greek model of Odysseus, who, with the help of his patroness Athena, manages to survive Troy and return home. Detienne and Vernant remark that both Platonism and Christianity have impeded the recognition of cunning intelligence as a universal virtue through their emphasis on Truth and the separation of humanity from the animal kingdom, a phenomenon especially illustrated in the development of meat eating in Greek society.

For Detienne, the myth of Prometheus is another wedge opening up the mysteries of Greek culture. It was Prometheus, as a Titan the predecessor of humanity, who not only stole fire from the Olympian gods but also proposed the division of animal sacrifice by use of chicanery: Prometheus tricked Zeus into accepting the contents of a bag (an ox's stomach) as the offering that humanity would give the gods for dividing up the animal kingdom. In the bag the entrails of the animals were reserved for the gods. Humans would have the flesh and fat as "leftovers." By hiding his gift to Zeus in a bag, Prometheus thus also became a model for cunning intelligence.

Woman is the third gift that Prometheus bestowed on men. Vernant, in an essay called "At Man's Table" (in his and Detienne's *The Cuisine of Sacrifice among the Greeks*), connects these gifts. Pandora, as the first woman, is Zeus' final response to the wiles of Prometheus. Utilizing Detienne's discoveries about the crucial role of sacrifice, Vernant succinctly observes that "sacrifice is the cornerstone of the religion of the city."[25]

Detienne's investigation into the myths of sacrifice have also led him to decipher the roles of the deviant cults in Greek society. The four major cults were the Dionysiac, the Orphic, the Pythagorean, and the Cynic. All were forms of social protest against the formation of the city. Their presence was subversive but also valuable in the drive for a model of the city-state. Their rituals and beliefs also allow Detienne to set up a framework for myths similar to the one advocated by Vernant: Detienne can show that "man's median position between beasts and gods is entrenched, buttressed by the entire politico-religious system ...."[26]

As we have seen in our hypothesized "Detiennian" view of Oedipus, the Dionysiac cult was divided into vines incarnated by Bacchus and the trance-like rites of madness, murder, and defilement represented by Dionysus. Detienne continues to argue that "there is no distance between the god of wine and the god of the trance"[27] in pointing to the divinity represented in the agora of Corinth by two identical statues to this god. Ceremonies involved wine and appealed to women to be his followers in orgiastic ceremonies of violence and drunkenness. Detienne discovers a tradition in Gaul in which women attendants to Dionysus were required to reconstruct the roof of his temple once a year. The roof had to be replaced in the course of a single day. During one of these activities a woman stumbled and fell while working. The others jumped on her, dismembered her, and then paraded around the temple carrying parts of her body. This two-part story, demonstrating Dionysus as the Roof-Building god and as the Stumbler inspiring murderous rage, supplies Detienne with another wedge in analyzing the bloody sacrifices found in Greek culture.

Orphic theology, evolving from the cult of Orpheus, claimed the rebirth of Dionysus after his violent death at the hands of the Titans. The Orphics claimed that the palpitating heart, with the leaping and spurting characteristic of Bacchic dances, was the source for the rebirth of this god. The resurrection of Dionysus was necessary to overcome the finality imposed by the Titans' murder. The Orphics were basically pacifists, drawing their doctrine from Orpheus' major doctrine: avoid murder. The rituals of this cult were also associated with a cereal diet and the avoidance of blood sacrifice. Combining Pythagoreanism, which was generally ascetic, with the Dionysiac religion, which sought possession of the human spirit, Orphism undercut the primacy of blood sacrifice as the primary means of approaching humanity and divinity within Greek society.

Finally, the Cynics, followers of Diogenes of Sinope (400-c. 325 B.C.), were a less philosophical group but were also subversive of social convention. Diogenes taught that anything that is natural is honorable and therefore should be done in public. This doctrine of shamelessness brought him the title of "dog." The word "cynic" is derived from this appellation. Within the spirit of the Cynics for naturalness Detienne explains the "elegantly immoral"[28] myths of Apollo as the purifier who dons a sacrificial knife to murder others in the name of cleansing. His priests at Delphi continue the act in his name as a ceremonial bloodletting and sacrifice imitating at once the wolf and Apollo.[29] The myths speak about a male butcher, sacrificer, and cook (*mageiros*) whose grammatical form has no feminine because the role is associated with the "natural" carnivorous and warrior-like traits associated with man and god, recalling the Golden Age when they both sat at the same table.

THE SHADOW OF HEIDEGGER

The connection between the German philosopher Martin Heidegger and Detienne is a commentary upon the politics of the Gernet School. Heidegger's brilliant thought was tarnished by his association with the Nazis during the 1930s. His involvement has been much debated, as has the question whether his politics should affect the assessment of his philosophy.[30] Some of Detienne's critics maintain that Detienne's decision to leave Heidegger's name out of his copious notes[31] despite the obvious influence exemplifies Detienne's "hostility toward philosophers."[32] Detienne is too careful a scholar to have overlooked the precedent provided by Heidegger. Doubtless he was influenced by Vernant's failure to mention Heidegger. Ironically, the decision to leave out Heidegger's name has fueled a controversy in itself!

The deeper issue is whether philology and philosophy are compatible in the analysis of myth. The collaboration of Vernant the philosopher and Detienne the philologist might seems to prove their compatibility. However, Robert Harrison, in his *Diacritics* review of Vernant and Detienne's works, notes that Vernant and Detienne's study of cunning

intelligence tends "to deprivilege the speculative drive of
Greek philosophy and to vindicate the practical nature of the
Greeks."[33] Much of the scholarship on myth from scholars
associated with the Gernet Center has likewise presented the
practical sense of myth as the expression of a cultural situation
rather than the projection of a philosophical or speculative
attitude.

This insight is especially applicable to Detienne's
reworking of Heidegger's presentation of Truth. In many ways
Detienne is doing what Heidegger would have done had he
been more of a philologist than a philosopher. The Greek
philosophers Parmenides (590-c. 460 B.C.) and Plato (c.429-
347 B.C.) used the word *aletheia* to refer to Truth. The
relationship of Truth to myth was especially invoked by Plato
in the previously cited question posed by Phaedrus: "Do you
believe that this talk about myth is true?" In the twentieth
century Heidegger responded to Phaedrus by linking the word
for Truth to *aletheia*, literally meaning "to uncover oblivion."
Many philologists contest Heidegger's idiosyncratic
appropriation of arbitrary links between "truth" and *aletheia*
and thus discredit Heidegger's philological scholarship, despite
recent claims that Heidegger has been right. In an apparent
justification of Heidegger's etymology Detienne points to the
evolution of the term *aletheia*. The rationalist Parmenides
reconciled the opposition between *lethe* ("oblivion") and
aletheia (in its meaning as "memory"): "There is not *aletheia* (+)
on the one side and *lethe* (-) on the other but instead an
intermediary zone between the two where *aletheia* slides
toward *lethe* and vice versa."[34] This "intermediary zone" is
where Heidegger located the "uncovering of oblivion," a
crucial concept in his systematic placement of Being (*Dasein*)
as the central issue of human existence. Yet Detienne makes
no mention of Heidegger, despite Heidegger's enormously
influential speculations on the pre-Socratic philosophers.

The shadow of Heidegger is especially marked in
Detienne's discussion of the "invention of mythology." Where
Heidegger proposed replacing metaphysics with ontology,
Detienne proposes replacing mythic reality with mythology
since mythology for him is a more encompassing concept

meaning the application of rational thought to *muthos*. Both substitutions, from metaphysics to ontology and from mythic reality to mythology, entail the replacement of abstraction by system. Although "it is so evident that a mythology without stories is unthinkable,"[35] there is no common agreement as to what myth really is: the form of the stories or the content involving the religious attitude, the belief in fables, and the narratives about gods and humanity. Detienne provides a chronology of the development of mythology around this *muthos*. But the core around which this study is concentrated may be oblivion. I am reminded of Heidegger's model for ontology in the *aletheia* which covers oblivion even as it discovers it: "The goddess of Truth who guides Parmenides puts two pathways before him, one of uncovering, one of hiding."[36] In his philological study of *aletheia* Detienne must have come across these words, which are echoed throughout Detienne's work. Myth and mythology are effectively two sides of the same coin, just as *muthos* and *logos* complement each other while remaining distinct.

In his pursuit of the cultural and mythological contexts for such concepts as *mètis*, *daîmon*, and *aletheia* Detienne also retraces the steps of Heidegger's reconciliation of historical precedents with the philosophical situation of *Dasein*. Detienne discovers that "*aletheia* is at the core of rational thought as one of the terms that most clearly indicates a certain line of continuity between religion and philosophy."[37] The religious issues are manifold and interspersed throughout myths. However, the relationship of Truth to time is the problem that occupies Heidegger.

Like the ambivalence that Heidegger sees operating in Parmenides' presentation of the term *aletheia*, Detienne sees the operations effected by it   for example, the opening and closing upon oblivion   as composing "a truth which is founded in and by dialogue."[38] Detienne proposes that dialogue take place between the contemporary structural analyst and the classical Greeks. Certainly the melding of structural insight with information about those past events opens a dialogue that engages us in the reconsideration of what time is. For Heidegger, time is *the* criterion by which we

understand the nature of our existence. However, the revealing
dialogue also produces a concomitant closing upon oblivion.
This closing has to do with Heidegger's *Destruktion*, which he
describes in answering the question, "What is Philosophy?":

> This path to the answer to our question is not a break
> with history, no repudiation of history, but is an
> adoption and transformation of what has been handed
> down to us. Such an adoption of history is what is
> meant by the term "destruction" (*Destruktion*) ...
> Destruction does not mean destroying but dismantling,
> liquidating, putting to one side the merely historical
> assertions about the history of philosophy. Destruction
> means—to open our ears, to make ourselves free for
> what speaks to us in tradition as the Being of being. By
> listening to this interpellation we attain the
> correspondence.[39]

Detienne likewise listens to the "interpellation" between
philosophy and history in order to arrive at "the
correspondence" with the classical Greeks that redefines our
conception of time.
    The concept of "correspondence" for Heidegger is linked
to an "event." The German word *Ereignis* means for him "the
coming of an event." Similarly, Detienne portrays the events
of classical antiquity as coming to us in the present by the
power of memory represented by the invention of mythology.
This narration of myths presents the past as past and the
present as the meaningful gathering of myths into bundles
relating to the modern reader. Heidegger even has a future in
mind as the projection of our lives go forward with the
meanings of events. Detienne, however, does not take that step
with Heidegger. Whereas Heidegger focuses on an apocalyptic
endpoint while strategically forgetting beginnings—the
Anaximander text is a palimpsest the original contexts of
which cannot be deciphered, thus assigning philosophy to a
destiny of "the process of trans-lation or trans-
scription"[40]—Detienne looks at the beginnings as retrievable

projections toward the present and beyond. An apocalyptic future is not within the scope of Detienne's structural analysis. Instead, the promises of change and development, as traced from the past through the present in the mythical event, bear witness to an ever-clearer movement. The light of human understanding grows brighter as we forget the former enlightenment of divine wisdom.

HUMAN AMNESIA AND DIVINE MEMORY

In the movement forward and backward from and toward the Greeks, Detienne discovers that their sense of memory is not so chronologically bound as the modern historical memory tends to be. Vernant presented the Greeks with a "deified memory"[41] not focused on reconstructing the past according to a time-line. The past was much more a question of human relationships to the gods and their intervention or nonintervention in human affairs. As the fables of the myths decreased in popularity because of the rising human civic order of the city, such a past did not bolster either confidence or stability. The myths, along with this sense of divine memory, were driven underground. In their wake a much more potent form of myth was engendered by the kinds of exclusions fostered in the civic model. Detienne proposes to map this model through the "silent myths" contained in the marginalized stories of the rejections and refusals by Greek society. The "silent myths" thus offer inroads into the culture by leading to concepts that formed the hidden bedrock of the society.

One of the "silent myths" for the Greeks was the presence of the *daîmon* between gods and humanity, between the *muthos* and the *logos*, and between religion and philosophy. Detienne exposed the evolution of this complex notion in 1958 in his thesis for the doctorat du IIIe cycle at the Sorbonne. The *daîmon* evolved from an exterior being to an interior sense of self—a parallel to the evolution among the Greeks from religious to philosophical Weltanschauungen. The Pythagoreans spoke about the souls of the dead as demons and later about the purification of one's own soul as the act of realizing one's *daîmon*—an intuitive sense of otherness obtained in self-reflection. This act was an effective way of separating soul from body. Detienne points out that the dualism of *daîmon* as exterior being and inner voice gave it a role as an intermediary between gods and humanity.[42] Humanity thus participated in the divine life to the degree that human behavior was attuned to this "silent myth."

The gods helped humanity in its pursuit of this alignment with the *daîmon*. Detienne illustrates this assistance with studies of how various divinities intervened in human projects. Athena, the patroness of Odysseus, became the "sea-crow" in order to inspire Odysseus and his crew in the construction and navigation of ships. Her patronage taught humanity "the art of the helmsman,"[43] of navigating through the waters of life. Apollo represents the paradoxical situation of sacrifice within Greek religious practices. He, the only Greek divinity portrayed in vase paintings with a knife raised above the head of his enemies, taught the lesson of the Dionysiac rituals: that violence and purification go hand in hand, so that "the excesses of murder are inseparable from the rigors of purity."[44] The external demon of the soul of the dead is thereby joined with the internal voice of the *daîmon*, whose otherness is celebrated in the purifying of the self.

The human celebration of the *daîmon* entails the silent myth of the marginalization of women in Greek society. Detienne reveals that women were not included in the various privileged relationships between god and humanity, especially in the rituals of sacrifice. Detienne cites Palladas, an epigrammatic poet of the fourth century A.D., who recalls the classical Greek values about the role of women thus:

> The woman is the anger of Zeus. She was given to us to make up for the fire. For a woman burns up her man through the worries she brings him, she consumes him and brings him premature old age.[45]

Although there was a theoretical equality between the sexes in Plato's *Republic*, Plato charged that women were inferior to men and were responsible for more than half the tasks that men should have performed. The ascetic Pythagoreans viewed women as synonymous with pleasure, softness, and sensuality. Women were thus viewed as a source of disorder in men's ascetic endeavor and the specific cause of political crises such as the one in the city of Croton at the end of the sixth century B.C. Economically, women were assigned to gardening and the gathering of fruit.

According to Vernant, all these efforts to keep women in their "place" were condoned by Hestia as goddess of the hearth. Detienne has discovered two complementary festivals in which women reversed the tables and excluded men from participating. The two festivals reflect the morality of woman's behavior viewed from the institution of marriage. Caring for the household was accepted as proper and acceptable behavior whereas the seductive and wily charms of the female seductress were improper and threatening to the common good. This dual role was incarnated in the festivals to the divinities Demeter and Adonis.

On the one hand the worship of Adonis promoted eroticism and seduction alongside marriage, and even within it. The Adonia were festivals in which single women invited married men to celebrate their sexuality. Married women were excluded. These festivals gave power to those women who, as unmarried, were marginal in society.

On the other hand the married women themselves had their own festival worshipping the corn goddess Demeter in rituals called the Thesmaphoria. Men were excluded from these ceremonies. Detienne relates a myth about Battus the Founder, the King of Cyrene, who enters the Thesmaphoria to discover women acting like ordinary men. He is attacked and castrated by the women of the festival. The festival itself creates an occasion for Greek wives to act out their frustrations. The killing of Battus is characteristic behavior for the "Demetrian Amazons," who celebrate their power in the center of the city, the heart of politics. Orphic legend tells that Orpheus was killed by angry women. Orphism thus rejected both women and sacrifice in its search for righteousness and purification. Aristophanes (c. 457-385 B.C.) illustrates the female acquisition of male power in his *Lysistrata* (411 B.C.), in which women act as transvestites with beards and cloaks to imitate men and take over the affairs of the city. These festivals purportedly occurred in Athens because, as Detienne explains, "the city of women is set up in the very space where the most specific virtues of the mature female sex are articulated: she is established, rooted in her status of lawful and fertile wife."[46] From that position the woman could make noise and shake up things. As the cities and demes (relationships among all classes and ranks based on geographic proximity) developed, women became priests and ministers, positions reserved in some cases wholly for women.

The Dionysian rituals combined the activities of the Adonia and the Thesmaphoria. As noted in the analysis of Oedipus, women were involved in constructing the temple to Dionysus and also as bacchante acting out the violent sacrifices denied to them in the usual practices of Greek religious purification. In the Dionysiac cult women acted out their fantasies of political and sexual power.[47]

Detienne has also discovered an undercurrent of feminist androgyny in Greek myths. In retaliation for Zeus' swallowing Mètis and then himself giving birth to Athena, his wife Hera becomes envious of his ability to reproduce parthenogenetically, or by himself. Detienne tells us that "Hera needs to invent an unknown drug"[48] and finally meets the goddess of blossoming plants Flora, who demonstrates that by brushing her skin along a floral pistil she can become pregnant. By the use of various plants Hera thus gave birth to Arès, the god of war, and Hephaestos, the smith-god. The Pythagoreans, who advocated various means to reduce sexual appetite, promoted androgyny as an alternative to the social codes of marriage. Myths of androgyny question the established roles of men and women in marriage. As Vernant has said,[49] Detienne's research suggests that marriage was not always respected in classical Greece. There is a need for a study of the evolution of the institution of marriage among the Greeks and of the role that myth played in that evolution.

For Detienne, myth does not simply reflect the values of the Greek city but is in dialectical relationship with it. Detienne seeks the "silent myths" of the city. The situation of Oedipus, for example, would be understood much differently in a climate which rejects the rule of the tyrant. Oedipus is thus a "tyrant," one of the words often recurring to describe the Sophoclean Oedipus. Detienne portrays the context for reading Oedipus' character in this way:

> Outside the frame of the city and the hierarchical structure with which it is linked, man, god, and beast are merely interchangeable objects of the tyrant's desires, which compel him to incest and patricide and finally to auto-cannibalism. In eating his own flesh and blood, the tyrant proclaims that he is outside the rules.[50]

Oedipus can thus be seen as "outside the rules" of the city and must perish as the pariah and scapegoat for a system seeking to escape from its mythical fables. Enter the historian: Pierre Vidal-Naquet, whose virtue and virtuosity have been to take Detienne's empirical categories to the planes where myth and history intersect.

NOTES

1. Marcel Detienne, *Dionysus Slain*, trs. Mireille and Leonard Muellner (Baltimore: Johns Hopkins University Press, 1979), p. ix.

2. In his and Vernant's *Cunning Intelligence in Greek Culture and Society* tr. Janet Lloyd (Atlantic Highlands [N.J.]: Harvester Press, 1978), p. 3, he describes their work "acting rather as archaeologists."

3. Detienne, *Dionysus Slain*, p. 9.

4. Robert A. Segal, review of Detienne's *The Creation of Mythology*, *Journal of the American Academy of Religion*, LVI, 1 (Spring 1988), p. 148.

5. Marcel Detienne, *Rethinking Mythology*, tr. John Leavitt (Chicago: University of Chicago Press, 1982), p. 43.

6. Marcel Detienne, *The Creation of Mythology*, tr. Margaret Cook (Chicago: University of Chicago Press, 1986), p. ix.

7. *Ibid.*, p. 1.

8. Detienne, *Dionysus Slain*, p. 2.

9. Marcel Detienne, "The Myth of 'Honeyed Orpheus'," in *Myth, Religion & Society*, ed. R. L. Gordon (Cambridge: Cambridge University Press, 1981), p. 109.

10. *Ibid.*, p. 12.

11. Marcel Detienne, *Dionysos at large*, tr. Arthur Goldhammer (Cambridge: Harvard University Press, 1989), p. 46.

12. *Ibid.*, p. 47.

13. *Ibid.*, p. 48.

14. See Marcel Detienne, *La Notion de Daïmôn dans le Pythagorisme Ancien* (Paris: Les Belles Lettres, 1963), and his and Vernant's philological analysis of *mètis* in their *Cunning Intelligence*, pp. 57-92.

15. Detienne, "The Myth of 'Honeyed Orpheus,'" p. 96.

16. *Ibid.*, p. 101.

17. Detienne, *Dionysus Slain*, p. 8.

18. Marcel Detienne, *The Gardens of Adonis*, tr. Janet Lloyd (Sussex: Harvester Press, 1977), p. 131.

19. Segal, on Detienne, p. 147.

20. Detienne, *Dionysus Slain*, p. 57.

21. Vernant, introd. to Detienne, *The Gardens of Adonis*, p. v.

22. My translation of Jean-Pierre Vernant, "Remarques," *Bulletin de la société française de philosophie*, LVI (1963), 17.

23. Detienne, "The Myth of 'Honeyed Orpheus'," p. 108.

24. Detienne and Vernant, *Cunning Intelligence*, p. 14.

25. Jean-Pierre Vernant, *Myth and Society in Ancient Greece*, tr. Janet Lloyd (New York: Zone Books, 1988), p. 176.

26. Detienne, "Between Beasts and Gods," in *Myth, Religion and Society*, ed. R. L. Gordon (Cambridge: Cambridge University Press, 1981), p. 219.

27. My translation of Marcel Detienne, "Dionysos en ses parousies: un dieu épidémique," in *L'Association Dionysiaque dans les Sociétés Anciennes* (Rome: Ecole française de Rome, 1986), p. 83.

28. Marcel Detienne, "Apollo's Slaughterhouse," tr. Anne Doueihi, *Diacritics*, XVI, 2 (Summer 1986), p. 53.

29. Marcel Detienne and Jesper Svenbro, "The Feast of the Wolves or the Impossible City," in *The Cuisine of Sacrifice among the Greeks*, eds. Detienne and Jean-Pierre Vernant, tr. Paula Wissing (Chicago: University of Chicago Press, 1989), pp. 149 ff.

30. See my discussion of Heidegger's and de Man's collaboration in my "Jacques Derrida's Response to the Call for Ethics," *International Journal of Moral and Social Studies*, 6 (Spring 1991), pp. 3-18.

31. For example, Detienne's 147-page monograph, *Les Maîtres de vérité dans la Grèce Archaïque* (Paris: Maspero, 1979), contains 614 notes exemplifying his considerable erudition and meticulousness.

32. Robert Pogue Harrison, "The Ambiguities of Philology," *Diacritics*, XVI, 2 (Summer 1986), p. 15.

33. *Ibid.*

34. *Ibid.*, p. 71.

35. My translation of Detienne, *L'Invention de la mythologie* (Paris: Gallimard, 1981), p. 240.

36. Martin Heidegger, *Being and Time*, tr. John Macquarrie and Edward Robinson (New York: Harper & Row, 1962), p. 265.

37. My translation of Detienne, *Les Maîtres de vérité*, p. 146.

38. *Ibid.*, p. 143.

39. Martin Heidegger, *What is Philosophy?* trs. W. Kluback and J. T. Wilde (New York: Twayne, 1958), pp. 69-71.

40. Herman Rapaport, *Heidegger and Derrida* (Lincoln: University of Nebraska Press, 1989), p. 29.

41. My translation of Detienne, *Les Maîtres de vérité*, p. 15.

42. See Detienne, *La Notion de Daïmôn dans le Pythagorisme Ancien*, p. 170.

43. Detienne, "The 'Sea-Crow,'" in *Myth, Religion and Society*, p. 20.

44. Detienne, "Apollo's Slaughterhouse," p. 53.

45. Detienne, *The Gardens of Adonis*, p. 177.

46. Detienne, "The Violence of Well-Born Ladies: Women in the Thesmaphoria," in his and Vernant's *The Cuisine of Sacrifice among the Greeks*, p. 145.

47. See Mary R. Lefkowitz, *Women in Greek Myth* (Baltimore: Johns Hopkins University Press, 1986), for an enlightened discussion of the threat of women's intelligence to men in Greek society. For additional discussions of women and their membership in ritualized groups to act out identities denied to them openly in their cultures, see I. M. Lewis, *Ecstatic Religion: A Study of Shamanism and Spirit Possession* (London: Routledge, 1971) and Victor W. Turner, *The Ritual Process: Structure and Anti-Structure* (Chicago: Aldine, 1969).

48. Marcel Detienne, "Potagerie des femmes ou comment engendrer seule," *Traverses*, V-VI (1976), p. 75.

49. Vernant, *Myth and Society in Ancient Greece*, pp. 182ff.

50. Detienne, "Between Beasts and Gods," p. 220.

Chapter Six

VIDAL-NAQUET: A FACTOTUM OF HISTORY

Lévi-Strauss speaks of himself as the *bricoleur*, the resourceful person adaptive enough to get inside the systems of myths and discover their coherence. Pierre Vidal-Naquet finds the Lévi-Straussian structuralist model to be a "heuristic instrument"[1] for *The Black Hunter* (1981) and a study written with Jacques Le Goff on Chrétien de Troyes' *Yvain* entitled "Lévi-Strauss en Brocéliande."

But as a historian Vidal-Naquet finds severe limitations to the art of the *bricoleur*. He rejects the structuralist method because of what he calls its "metaphysical assumptions"—its assumption of a "structure" independent of the specific interactions among a culture, its myths, and the proponents of those myths. The "resourceful ingenuity" of *bricolage*, as presented by Lévi-Strauss, does not include the historian's craft of accounting for changes in myths over time. Lévi-Strauss sees his method as an alternative to historical concerns about time and makes no effort to integrate temporal changes into the method of *bricolage*.

By contrast, Vidal-Naquet proposes that a structural method can be adapted to "history." Myths become a culture's memory of what it is. While Vernant adapts psychology and philosophy to present myths as humanly functional stories, and while Detienne prefers a philological dialogue in which myth solves issues about semantic horizons, Vidal-Naquet portrays myths as instruments for the accurate human recollection of the past. Vidal Naquet thus applies "structural analysis" as a hybrid uniting structuralist connections with respect for the past.

113

Unlike the other members of the Gernet Center, Vidal-Naquet, the present Director, does not restrict his studies of myths to the classical Greeks. He carefully exposes stories proposed as myths in order to cover up the truth. The invented stories are not myths themselves but rather substitutes made for the sake of ideologies. Vidal-Naquet has sought to reveal the false presentations of French justice regarding individual rights, class conflicts, and the humane treatment of others. He seeks to reconstruct the context within which a "false story" is presented as a myth—a narrative passed on from one generation to another to preserve a human truth. Having lost his parents at Auschwitz, he is a Jew committed to debunking the recent "revisionist" attempts to downplay the effects of the Holocaust. He is a detective continually seeking to reveal facts about the past. As a seeker of facts about the past, he portrays himself "as a historian ... uncomfortable with the idea that there might be something definitive."[2] For example, he discovers myths found in Greek society that have been ignored or rejected by Greek tragedy.[3] In this role he would be a "socio-archaeologist," thus adding to his multi-disciplinary talents in the service of history and the structural method. I call Vidal-Naquet a factotum of history because he uses multiple talents to become a practitioner of *polichilia*,[4] meaning diversity and variety.

Contrary to the philosophical stance of Vernant's "mythology," which gives a context to a myth, but compatible with Detienne's "silent myths" which point to the underlying knowledge of a culture, myths for Vidal-Naquet do portray the past, but they do so selectively and imperfectly. Whereas the Greek tradition of *logos* tended to assign all myths to fabulous narratives, Vidal-Naquet carefully separates the ideologically motivated aspects of myths from the truth. By placing myth in its ideological setting, he promotes the adage that "history recognizes, and within certain limits, contains political conflict."

The implementation of this adage was especially exemplified by Vidal-Naquet's mentor and Cambridge model, classicist Moses Finley. The Cambridge connection was inspirational for Vidal-Naquet. From Finley he learned to question and find breaks in the logics of accepted ways of thinking about history. The Cambridge Philological Society, with Finley and Edmund Leach at its helm, first acclaimed Vidal-Naquet's theory of "the black hunter" in 1968, even before the French recognized its significance as the first structural study by a classical Greek historian.

Just as Finley's method pointed out flaws in traditional theories about the Greeks and the Romans, Vidal-Naquet took exception to the French Government's presentation of the Algerian War from 1954 to 1962. Vidal-Naquet has long been involved in exposing the coverups about the atrocities in Algeria and thus revealing "the great Algerian lie"[5]. He was suspicious about cracks in the seams of official reports about the Algerian War. In *L'Affaire Audin* (1958) he debunked the Government's denial that the military arrested and strangled the mathematics professor Maurice Audin. In *La Torture dans la république* (1972) he analyzed the crisis for democracy revealed by the condoning of atrocities. In *Les Crimes de l'armée française* (1975) he provided eyewitness accounts and documents of the atrocities. Vidal-Naquet's studies of Algeria reminded him of another racially divided era in French history: "I had the Dreyfus Affair as a background when I entered, not without illusions, the debates that marked the Algerian Affair."[6] The racism he encountered along the way clouded the "truth" with the myths of justice that the French Government wanted the French people to believe. The Algerian Affair had many folds and layers of true and false beliefs in its narrative. As a historian, Vidal-Naquet isolated the layers and their folds to demonstrate "the work of a historian as a kind of stripping operation."[7]

The "stripping operation" of Vidal-Naquet the historian has allowed him to separate truth from error and lies. "Truth" is not easily separated from what people want to believe. Vidal-Naquet learned that there was a myth that the system of French justice was right. That myth had to be examined more closely because mass hysteria had woven prejudices into the fabric of the story to victimize such innocent people as Alfred Dreyfus, Maurice Audin, and Luc Tangorre, this latter person sacrificed to a public outcry against serial crimes of rape

during the 1980s. Vidal-Naquet learned from his involvement
in these three cases that: " ... all the legal arms from the Court
of Appeals to councils of war are incapable of arriving at the
complete truth if the French conscience doesn't demand daily
accounts of the whole truth."[8]

Being a watchdog over truth and justice requires an eye
for inconsistencies in historical documents. Vidal-Naquet
admits that this activity is fraught with traps because "what is
off-putting about error is precisely its resemblance to truth."[9]
However, he is undaunted in his drive to identify the fictional
component of myth and to isolate the factual basis for the
ideological spinning of a tale. This is his contribution to the
structural method. He is the audacious investigator using the
structural method in his constant verification of the facts with
which myths are constructed.

Even more crucial, however, is the quality that the
classicist Bernard Knox sees in Vidal-Naquet's *The Black
Hunter*: audacity "tempered and checked by the historical
conscience."[10] That conscience is an ethical responsibility
that Vidal-Naquet shoulders as a historian confronting myths.
Myths are palimpsests of the past, documents in which texts
have been written over numerous times with the prior versions
imperfectly erased. Within these palimpsests that are myths,
Vidal-Naquet delineates ethical judgments that were made
regarding the retention of certain versions or the correction of
others for future generations.

FACE TO FACE WITH MYTHS

The French philosopher Emmanuel Lévinas (b. 1905)
speaks about ethics as an acceptance of the responsibility for
meeting others face to face. Vidal-Naquet fulfills this ethical
responsibility as history confronts myth to challenge the
existence of myth as the repository for the collective memory
of a political unit.

Vidal-Naquet's structuralist analysis of Chrétien de
Troyes' *Yvain ou le chevalier au lion* (c. 1180) exemplifies this
positioning of a story within a political setting. He uses the
model of the Asdiwal analysis by Lévi-Strauss as the basis for

assuming the collective memory of a political group within a myth. A myth thus recollects the past for a particular group in a particular political manner. While the Asdiwal myth for Lévi-Strauss incorporates the political intersection of the Tsimshian and Nisqa Indians in his ethnographical context, for Vidal-Naquet politics is found in the ideological choices of the narrator. Yvain, the hero, must choose one of the debated methods of warfare at the time: either the bow and arrow or face-to-face, hand-to-hand combat. Yvain chooses face-to-face combat: "For a warrior, the test of bravery is not pulling a bow; it consists in remaining at your post and in seeing, without blinking or being distracted, a whole field of lances aimed right at you, while you maintain your position."[11]

For Vidal-Naquet, this myth is the collective memory of the soldier engaged in combat as representative of the political group, that is the military, in its self-image of heroism. Vidal-Naquet recasts myths as political and ideological encounters being debated by the contemporaries of the story. As Nicole Loraux has pointed out,[12] the word "confrontation," often used by Vidal-Naquet in his description of myths and their political settings, appropriately characterizes his insights as well as his method.

In his face-to-face encounters with myths as ideological settings Vidal-Naquet typically sees political issues as subtexts. For example, his presentation of Plato's myth of the statesman demands discussion of the subversive activities of the Cynics. The statesman myth, narrated in Plato's *Laws* by Socrates to the stranger from Elea, portrays the statesman as the shepherd of the human flock. Vidal-Naquet claims that the "human flock" was not, in fact, homogeneous in the fourth century B.C., for the Cynics were inciting crises with their advocacy of eating raw food and practicing masturbation, incest, and cannibalism. The problem for the statesman is that, although the politically minded leader can create the illusions of harmony between science and happiness, between religion and the city, and between history and daily life, there will always be a breach represented by the conjunction "and." Myths often hide the lies of such illusory political ties by their apparently naive stories. In his efforts to retrieve the hidden political conjunctions, Vidal-Naquet points to the notion of "the irreconcilable"[13] in the fifth century B.C. as an indicator of the pessimistic view of humanity caught in the breaches of ambiguity. The politician was pretending that the city could resolve all conflict. Plato set up the ambiguous values of history that the rhetoric of the City's statesman then falsely harmonized to give the illusion of homogeneity among the Greeks. It promised the possible return to a Golden Age.

The Golden Age serves Vidal-Naquet as a metaphor for what has happened to the true test of "time" in the history of classical Greece. Time is fictionalized and becomes too rigid, somewhat like the four metals Hesiod uses to describe the ages of humanity. Instead, Vidal-Naquet proposes that classical Greece be understood as a succession of cycles in which there were breaks in cosmology such as the one between history as storytelling and history as science begun in the fifth century by Thucydides. The linear succession of moments as historical time was an ideological justification for the sense of promise and fulfillment accorded to Judeo-Christian thought[14] and thus restricts our understanding of Greek culture to passing through such a time line. Of course, this fluid order must rest upon the crucial task of the historian, who, like Odysseus, " ... constantly remembers ... the true man who stands out from his forgetful companions."[15] Vidal-Naquet himself is such a true man. He jars memories with unusual facts that make us rethink events. He seeks "to bring into dialogue that which does not naturally communicate according to the usual criteria of historical judgment."[16] Let us now examine the Oedipus myth to see how he does this.

OEDIPUS AS URBAN STRANGER

Vidal-Naquet shows us an Oedipus victimized by the rising tide of the Greek city-state. Homer has Oedipus die while King of Thebes, but Aeschylus and Sophocles transform Oedipus into what Vidal-Naquet calls "a self-blinded exile."[17] Sophocles presents Oedipus within a tragic cycle of three plays: *Oedipus Rex, Oedipus at Colonus,* and *Antigone.*

According to Vidal-Naquet, these three tragedies were staged for a Greek populace struggling with the limits of the city's power. Oedipus is the incarnation of the Other, the one who does not conform to the laws of the city. His eventual downfall is predictable because he is the foreigner, the noncitizen, who has a privileged status above all the other natives and residents of the city.

The Athenians had a tradition for adolescent males (*ephebeia*) to go through certain rites of passage before they were accepted as citizens of the city. Vidal-Naquet portrays this political setting as providing the collective truths of certain Greeks myths providing selective memory for these rites of passage into Athenian society. In *The Black Hunter*, and in his earlier essay on the topic, Vidal-Naquet documents the political ideology of the Spartan military training as one of these rites of passage (*krypteia*). Adolescent males were left on the hinterland of the city to demonstrate their ability to survive while guarding the city's frontiers. In several essays on the Sophoclean Oedipus published in *Myth and Tragedy in Ancient Greece*[18] Vidal-Naquet argues that this presentation of Oedipus is a tragic story of frontiers. As a child, Oedipus is left on the hinterland of Mt. Cithaeron, described by the Greek chorus of *Oedipus Rex* as "the wild frontier that separates Thebes and Athens"—a land that is "native to him."[19] Since the "frontier" is native to Oedipus, he will always be a foreigner in the cities of Thebes and Athens. Vidal-Naquet claims that in *Oedipus at Colonus* "Colonus is a miniaturized, condensed Athens."[20] Oedipus struggles to be accepted by the citizenry, but from the beginning he is "a misguided ephebe,"[21] never to be fully accepted.

Similar to the geographically oriented history of Fernand Braudel, one of the founders of the *Annales* School of history, Vidal-Naquet orients our reading of the Sophoclean Oedipus through the situation of Thebes and Athens. These cities become the polarized centers attracting or repelling Oedipus according to the political and religious criteria of the tragic spectacle. While Thebes is the anti-city because of its division by civil war and its tyrannical ruler Creon, Athens (Colonus) is the ideal, unified city thanks to the leadership under the sanction of law by Theseus and his capability for "mobilizing all its citizens, hoplites [traditional Greek foot-soldiers] and cavalry alike, in the service of a just cause."[22] These points of reference are crucial. Vidal-Naquet says that "the organization of symbolic space does not always coincide with actual geography."[23] The ramifications of the politics and ideology situating Oedipus have far more importance than the mere location of Oedipus within a physical space.

Vidal-Naquet reminds us that the setting for the spectacle provided the ambiance for judging the tragedy of Oedipus. The altar of Dionysus, the *thymelé*, was at the center of the circular orchestra. The chorus resided in front of the stage. As Dionysus was "the god who, of all the Olympians, was the one most foreign to the city."[24] The spectators had a visual reminder of the presence of the foreigner in the midst of the chorus which provided "a collective truth, an average truth, the truth of the city."[25] The collective truth is not, however, the whole truth. The spectators themselves judged Oedipus according to whether they could identify themselves with him.

The process of identification with a tragic figure entailed making the spectator aware of what was already known but not necessarily discussed among Greeks. Vidal-Naquet says that the known involved the communal understanding of *oikos*, a word meaning "family," "home," "parents," "children," and also "slaves." He presents Antigone caught up in the ambivalence of this word as she struggles to express her loyalty to her brother, who was mindful of the city's laws (Eteocles), or to her brother who died attacking the city (Polynices). Likewise Oedipus projects an ambivalence toward "family." Does Polybus have a stake in fatherhood after Laius rejects Oedipus? Is Merope rather than Jocasta his true mother? Politically, should Thebes or Colonus be called "his cities"? For Vidal-Naquet, Oedipus resides in between his two fathers, mothers, and cities. The ostracism and *pharmakos*, discovered by Vernant as political and religious instruments applied on the tragic stage, reflect Sophocles' own situation of the foreigner within the context of the city.

Vidal-Naquet realizes that the opposition of foreigner to the citizen was a problematic one in the daily life of the "parents," "children," and also "slaves." He presents Antigone caught up in the ambivalence of this word as she struggles to express her loyalty to her brother, who was mindful of the city's laws (Eteocles), or to her brother who died attacking the city (Polynices). Likewise, Oedipus projects an ambivalence toeard "family." Does Polybus have a stake in fatherhood after Laius rejects Oedipus? Is Merope his true mother rather than Jocasta, as some, including Vernant, have reiterated in response to Freud's decision to make Jocasta the basis for the triangular complex? Politically, should Thebes or Colonus be called "his cities"? For Vidal-Naquet, Oedipus resides in between his two fathers, mothers, and cities. The ostracism and *pharmakos*, discovered by Vernant as political and religious instruments applied on the tragic stage, reflected Sophocles' own situation of the foreigner within the context of the city.

Vidal-Naquet realizes that the opposition of foreigner to the citizen was a problematic one in the daily life of the Greeks. Oedipus was not, however, simply a foreigner. In Colonus, he became a resident and a "privileged metic."[26] A "metic" was a resident alien in a Greek city. The status of "alien" always made Oedipus a marginal figure even when he was recognized as a hero and given honorary citizenship in Colonus. The citizens of Thebes excluded him and requested his return in order to treat him as a criminal, once again an outsider marginalized from membership in any city because he belonged to no family. Politically and religiously, Oedipus occupied a "frontier no-man's land."[27]

The citizen/foreigner context was a spatial problem in the staging of the Sophoclean Oedipus. The problem had political and religious ramifications for the Greek city and for the role of the individual within or outside the laws of the city. Hence Vidal-Naquet is concerned with the staging of Oedipus. The organization of the dramatic space was an allegory for the political and religious frontiers of the Greek city-state. The *bema*, a step or a raised platform on the Greek stage, provided the geographical separation of Oedipus from the citizenry as a result of his ostracism and treatment as a scapegoat. After studying several variations of the Sophoclean Oedipus over the centuries Vidal-Naquet returns to his original premise of "the political problem posed by this series of adaptations, namely the problem of power."[28] While Lévi-Strauss connects Oedipus in an elaborate series of structural relationships to his past and both Vernant and Detienne connect Oedipus with his setting, Vidal-Naquet views the disconnectedness of Oedipus as reflective of the political tensions in the Greek City. Oedipus never had power because he was always in-between, on the frontiers, never allowed to belong to his family. And likewise, the Greek City was the scene for much debate about who belonged and did not belong to its power base.

MILITANT MYTHS

The frontier has always interested Vidal-Naquet in his quest for clarifying the roles of subversives and marginalized groups. He has sought to determine the line between truths and lies in his studies of the myths surrounding the Algerian War, the 1968 student revolts in Paris, the Diaspora of the Jews, and the Luc Tangorre affair. In these involvements of myth and history Vidal-Naquet does not go so far as to call myths sheer lies. Rather, myths are historically developed tales in which there is a mixture of reporting and invention. Vidal-Naquet the historian breaks down that mixture. He delineates where the myths have seduced us into believing both their truths and their fictions.

Vidal-Naquet's commitment to revealing coverups in the Algerian War was the beginning of a career dedicated to the exposure of the political roots of myths. Maurice Audin was a mathematics professor in Algiers arrested in June 1956 by French paratroopers and then strangled during interrogation. The French Government had denied that these events ever happened. Vidal-Naquet revealed not only the veracity of the incident but also the systematic use of torture by the French military in Algeria. His book *L'Affaire Audin* (1958) brought the case to trial in 1966, became the basis for the Audin Committee and resulted in the legal admission of the facts in 1970.

Meanwhile Vidal-Naquet pursued the problem of the official sanctioning of torture by the military in Algeria. He collected Government documents that sanctioned torture and in 1962 published them in a pamphlet called *La Raison d'Etat* (The Government's Reasoning: Why We Are Here). In 1963, he published in English *Torture: Cancer of Democracy*. It appeared in French in 1972. He also gathered eyewitness accounts and incriminating documents on the atrocities of the Algerian War in *Les Crimes de l'armée française* in 1975. Together with other French intellectuals, he called for a halt to torture. This collective effort led to the 1961 Manifesto of the 121, in which intellectuals signed their names to a demand for action addressed to President de Gaulle. The solidarity of the French intellectuals helped to bring an end to the Algerian War as well as to sensitize the public to the reality of the military effort there.

In 1968 Vidal-Naquet once again aligned himself with subversive forces. Along with history student Alain Schnapp, who later became an archaeologist, he taped the opinions of students involved in trying to loosen the overly structured curriculum of French university students. Vidal-Naquet and Schnapp then gathered the transcripts of the tapes into a volume (*Journal de la commune* [1969], *French Student Uprising* [1971]) which dramatically presents the ideals and frustrations of those who rebelled. Once again, Vidal-Naquet the historian was determined to show the real drama behind "this *on* [the third person impersonal pronoun in French similar to the regal "we"] which was appearing as the mythical transposition of the technocratic system ...."[29] Like the French bureaucracy that created the students' outmoded curriculum, the students were being relegated to an impersonal realm by the Government even as they revolted. In reaction, Vidal-Naquet chose texts which "had the students themselves talk"[30] and thus present their side of the politically motivated myths about the "radical, left-wing" demonstrations.

Vidal-Naquet's project of exposing lies found in myth continues in his ongoing rebuttal of revisionist versions of anti-Semitism. "Revisionist" groups attempt to minimize the effects of anti-Semitism—above all by denying the Holocaust.

Vidal-Naquet participates in the "resistance" to forgetting anti-Semitism and separating lies from facts. For example, there have been several recent attempts to reduce the number of six million Jews lost in the Holocaust by pointing to the other groups at which Hitler's Final Solution was aimed. Vidal-Naquet notes the importance of maintaining vigilance over those facts so that future generations are not misled by "revisionist" presentations.

In 1981, he collected three studies and three prefaces in a work entitled *Les Juifs: la mémoire et le présent* (The Jews: The Past Remembered and the Present). Especially noteworthy is an essay in this collection on the "Masada complex", to which Vidal-Naquet returns in several prefaces to major works on the history of the Jews. The "Masada complex" refers to the mass suicide by Jewish defenders of the fortress against Rome. Masada itself is a large promontory, as imposing in the desert as the celebrated Rock of Gibraltar is in the Mediterranean. The "complex" is the supposed tendency of Jews to be self-defensive. It is the sense of being threatened by a surrounding wall which separates them from extermination. Vidal-Naquet admirably separates fact from fiction and rebuts various "myths" held by Jews themselves about the "Masada complex." He insists that "you have to understand that the fact of Masada is a complex relationship between a story and a site that can be neither separated nor superimposed one on the other."[31]

Vidal-Naquet also continues his campaign to maintain the memory of the Dreyfus Affair as a reminder of the hysteria that can be produced by lies and prejudices. He has written several articles and prefaces on Alfred Dreyfus, a Jewish captain in the French Army who was accused of treason in 1898. Dreyfus became a scapegoat for military officials and then a public scapegoat for fears that the Jews were more loyal to their religion than to the nation. Vidal-Naquet would have us reread Léon Blum's *Souvenirs sur l'affaire* (Memories of the [Dreyfus] Affair) from 1935 to remember the devotion to separating truth from fact even during those days of mass hysteria influenced by nationalist as well as racial prejudices.

An example from the July 1898 trial will suffice. After the lawyer Cavaignac told the Chamber of Deputies that the dossier on Dreyfus had convinced him of the guilt of Alfred Dreyfus, Jean Jaurès, a socialist deputy and defender of Dreyfus, replied:

> I swear to you that what Cavaignac just cited is false. These documents smell like lies and stink like them. These are false documents, stupidly fabricated to cover other lies. I am certain only upon hearing this [Cavignac's beliefs] and I'm going to prove it.[32]

This testimony by Jaurès serves as an admirable example of the responsibility that historians have toward myths assumed to be absolutely truthful. Were it not for Jaurès' determination to get to the facts in the case of Dreyfus, Dreyfus would be remembered as a traitor.

More recently, Vidal-Naquet has turned to the myth of the French legal system. His nephew first told him about Luc Tangorre, who had been accused of raping fifteen women in Marseilles from 1979 to 1981. Public hysteria put pressure on the police to find the criminal. Tangorre was convicted because he resembled sketches of the accused and had a kitchen knife in his possession. Gisèle Tichané put together a dossier that became a pamphlet. Vidal-Naquet wrote the afterward in which he exposed the sloppiness of the prosecutors in their investigation. For example, they had not tried on Tangorre the gloves left behind by the rapist of the first victim. Vidal-Naquet noted that "the prosecution had not proven the guilt of Luc Tangorre."[33] Once again, myth was a mixture of facts, prejudice, and error.

PARENTHESES IN THE CITY

The disfranchised members of the Greek city-states have also attracted the attention of the ethically-minded Vidal-Naquet. He specifically sees similarities between the treatment of slaves and the treatment of women in both Sparta and

Athens. Although slaves and women had political power,
neither was a citizen with a right to vote. Both groups were
feared by Greek men because of their numbers.

Vidal-Naquet points out that Plato and Aristophanes gave
women a social status at least equal to that of men. However,
both writers were making a fiction of the actual situation of
women in the city. Within Greek myths women were
denigrated by the story of Pandora, who was given to males by
Zeus as retribution for the tricks that Prometheus had played
on the gods. Pandora was presented as a scourge for mankind
to be passed on through womankind.

As Greek culture began to prefer *logos* to *muthos*, and as
the city-state was being planned and organized, the existing
role of women was simply transferred to the new systems.
Within the democratic city she was still not a citizen and still
had no vote. In Sparta the citizens actually feared civil war
from the women. Women were restricted to operating the
household. In Athens women had no vote and no rights to pass
their names on to their children. The condition was similar to
that of Greek slaves.

In Sparta those men who did not fight in the first
Messenian War (eighth century B.C.) were disfranchised from
the city and were given slave status with the title of *helots*.
These slaves, or *helots*, became useful throughout Greece. War
thus provided justification for increasing the numbers of those
with second-class status. Slaves joined the lot of Greek women
in being refused citizenship. In addition, Messenia was also the
site for a later uprising by the helots, so that the fear of their
revolt was also justified by a specific event. That fear justified
the denial of citizenship and even allowed the use of torture:
"The Greek City-State had the logical answer when it refused
to admit that slaves were human beings ...."[34] If slaves were
less than human beings, then they could be treated
inhumanely.

Both slaves and women were feared. As a consequence,
the city-states invented various laws to limit their power and
to control their freedom of movement. Ironically, as Vidal-
Naquet indicates, both slaves and women were also a source of
power for Greek men.[35] While the slaves were a measure of

a landowner's "servile interregnum" (Aristotle, *Poetics*, 5.3.7), women ensured the continuation of the species. Vidal-Naquet points out that in Athens, despite the matriarchal power implied by naming the city after the goddess Athena, Athenian children could not be known by their mother's name. The result was that "in the classical city there are no 'women of Athens' only wives and daughters of the 'men of Athens'."[36] Whereas it is widely acknowledged that oligarchic Sparta had a reputation as "the male city par excellence,"[37] even democratic Athens was dominated by a male society.

Technology was also responsible for the treatment of the fiction of Pandora as historical truth. The Greek development of *logos* also entailed respect for *technè*, which means both art, as in the art of getting rich, and trade, as in the trade of a sculptor or a banker. Vidal-Naquet defines *technè* as "anything which makes use of instruments (including living instruments like slaves)."[38] One of the byproducts of this technological awareness was the subjugation of others. Women were most clearly "other" for Greek men, who could justify their actions through the fiction of Pandora.

Meanwhile the city-state was creating its myth of a technologically oriented society, with distinct places for those who controlled the instruments and for those who were controlled. While the term "barbarian" described the foreigners, it could as well have been applied to slaves and women, who became instruments of the dominant ideology of a cultural and social ethos known as the Greek city-state.

The exception is curious yet understandable: "The Greek city, that men's club, had included in its catalogue of opposites an exclusively feminine kingdom, that of the Amazons."[39] As mythological female warriors, the Amazons represented women different from Greek women by wielding their own instruments (of warfare in their case) and thus retaining their own sense of technological integrity, apart from the male, Greek sense of *technè*.

Vidal-Naquet and Pierre Lévêque show that the Athenian Constitution was reformed to destroy kin-based social patterns and to insert mathematically based principles of *isonomia*, or equality before the law. Since Cleisthenes, the theoretician of

Athenian democracy, was a geometer, he deemed mathematics free of the prejudices of socially derived principles of government: "Under the law of *isonomia*, the social universe assumes the form of a circular or central *cosmos* wherein every citizen, similar to all the others, will be able to share in all the privileges ...."[40] These principles could not, however, overcome the prejudices of *muthos*, by which the second-class status of Pandora was a historical condition in Athens and Sparta.

FIGHTING OUTSIDE THE CITY

The antithesis of male and female was also strong in the Greek treatment of adolescents. Vidal-Naquet concentrates on the way Spartans and Athenians prepared their male youths for military service. He considers his analysis to be "the first endeavor ... by a Greek historian to use specifically, if critically, Lévi-Straussian concepts to understand some features of ancient Greek society."[41] Vidal-Naquet uses some data from myths collected cross-culturally, as did Lévi-Strauss, to study the Greek politics of the adolescent. He discovers that *ephebeia* is a semantic category in the sense of a Lévi-Straussian "symbolic operator." Vidal-Naquet's main critique of Lévi-Strauss is that the ethnologist's concerns for the myths of cultures with oral histories must be distinguished from the politics and ideologies of societies with written histories. The similarities between the two methods are that they both make connections among data not easily related. Vidal-Naquet thus calls the structuralist method of Lévi-Strauss "heuristic." However, Vidal-Naquet calls his own approach a "structural method" to distinguish it from that of "structuralism."

The term "black hunter" was invented by Vidal-Naquet to describe the conjunction of a particular set of myths, ceremonies, festivals, and traditions. The word "black" refers at once to the black cloak of the Athenian ephebe, to the young Athenian frontier fighter Melanthos ("the Black"), to an adolescent character Melanion in Aristophanes' *Lysistrata* (411

B.C.), and to the night ambushes of Spartan *kryptoi* (the adolescent initiates into the military). The word "hunter" describes the function of these adolescent rites: to teach males to be aggressive pursuers in war and in Greek life itself.

The myths of Melanthos and Melanion were connected to specific festivals in Greek culture. Melanthos is the basis for the Apaturia festival, in which there were initiation rites for young men. Just as young men everywhere often mimic behavior in total contrast to that expected of them as mature men, so the initiation rites were characterized by guile, disorder, individual performance, acting out as girls, and nighttime activities. Melanthos ("the Black") was an Athenian youth who led the defeat of the Boeotians by killing their king, Xanthos ("the Blonde"), through deceit. Melanthos distracted Xanthos with cries that someone else was next to him. As Xanthos turned to look, he was struck down by Melanthos. In the Apaturian festivals some Athenian youths wear black capes to commemorate and to imitate heroism achieved through trickery.

Melanion is celebrated by the chorus of old men in Aristophanes' *Lysistrata* as another black youth celebrated for his hunting with snares. This black lived in the mountains, where he deliberately lived to escape the congress of women. He was revered for his ability to hunt with traps and nets. Vidal-Naquet notes, however, that Melanion was a failed ephebe because he never got to the other side of the initiation rites of the ephebe. Melanion, like Adonis, was the eternal ephebe hero who never grew up and entered the commerce of men and women.

Vidal-Naquet also finds a link between "black" and deception in the Greek festival of Oschoporia, a celebration of the return of the young Theseus from his exploits in Crete. Aegeus, the father of Theseus, agreed upon his return to use a white sail to indicate his safety. Theseus forgot and flew a black sail instead. The black sail so disheartened Aegeus that he committed suicide. The Athenian ephebes commemorated this event with a black cloak during the festival of Oschoporia. In this case black was an ambivalent color signifying both the return of Theseus and his father's suicide due to the unwitting deception. Although deception had tragic consequences in this case, guile and the color black were connected in the example of a heroic youth. The use of deception was often advocated for ephebes. The Spartan practice of *krypteia* likewise required adolescent Greeks to set ambushes, traps, and snares to catch helots who were traveling the frontiers, in the wild hills, and often at night. This skill, noted as indicative of the virtue of *mètis* by Vernant and Detienne, is characteristic of the "black hunter" motif and is contrasted to the military skills usually needed by the typical mature soldier among the Greeks, the brute warrior known as the "hoplite." The hoplite usually fought during the day, collectively in groups known as the phalanx, and used traditional weapons such as the spear and the sword to combat opponents. The contrast between the ephebe and the mature soldier is that between night and day, ruse and face-to-face, individual and collective, order and disorder.

This last opposition between order and disorder needs explanation. While the battles of the hoplites were usually staged in a planned fashion and hence were representative of an ordered military style, the *kryptoi* were encouraged to use stealth to survive on the frontier. Vidal-Naquet stresses that these various rites of the ephebe were only transitory. The *kryptoi* even took an oath of allegiance to the hoplites as a sign that he would soon act totally differently.

Vidal-Naquet continues to make brilliant connections among the various exemplars of "the black hunter" in Greek society. He analyzes the role of the ephebe in Sophocles' *Philoctetes* (409 B.C.), in Homer's work, and throughout the politics of ancient Greek society. Although "the black hunter" has been well received by Sir Moses Finley and Sir Edmund Leach at Cambridge University, it has also been called "mystification"[42] by two professors at the University of Pisa. Bernard Knox, the eminent American classicist, has probably given the fairest indication of what the "black hunter" is: "exactly what the connection is between the black ephebic cloak, Melanthos the tricky fighter, and Melanion the woman-hating hunter may be disputed but that there is such a connection few readers of this book [Vidal-Naquet's *The Black Hunter*] can doubt."⁴³

The idiosyncratic connections of "the black hunter" are in fact not so arbitrary as Knox suggests. The ephebe, prepared in wily stratagems, could more effectively serve in the army when it was engaged in unpredictable battles and the chaos of warfare. Not only was Sparta a military power, but Athens in the fourth century B.C. was also, according to Vidal-Naquet, "entirely dedicated to being a promoter of war."⁴⁴

Vidal-Naquet has provided other insights into the assumptions about the Greek political reality behind the military. For example, he does not simply accept the notions of the honorable Homeric duel or the anonymous phalanx as the two great military accomplishments of the Greeks. On the one hand (in an introduction to a French edition of the *Iliad*) Vidal-Naquet asserts that the Homeric duel is a fiction. The promotion of one-on-one contests was ideological heroism to present the ideals of the opposing sides, but it could not settle wars which involved the forces of whole armies and weapons.

At the same time the anonymous phalanx became "another fiction."⁴⁵ It was a tactic used by the Greek hoplites in combat. The success of the phalanx depended on the collective cooperation of each soldier locking in his shield with the equipment of the soldier to his side. This tactic could be overcome in the disorder of battle. The individual hoplite was subject to the vagaries and uncertainties of warfare when the wall of shields crumbled.

The *ephebeia* was an institution in Greek life to introduce the marginalized child into the mainstream of mature male Greek society. Like the slaves, women, foreigners, and artisans (who will be discussed in chapter eight)⁴⁶, the child was an outcast of Greek city life. Vidal-Naquet explains how male children crossed the frontier from the margins into full citizenship:

> The trials and rites of adolescence situate the young Greek male outside the city, even outside the territorial limits, in a real or symbolic frontier-zone

where in its extreme anything is permitted, even
behavior which would in 'ordinary' times and places
would be called bestial or monstrous.[47]

The institution of *ephebeia* thus allowed the male child to act
totally other, within an accepted ritual, in order to make the
transition into the dominant political and ideological group.
Plato and Aristotle ally hunting with the political arts.
Aristotle defines a human being as the *zoon politikon*,
described by Vidal-Naquet as "a being living within the
city."[48] Vidal-Naquet adds hunting as the occasion to use the
structural method by complicating the bifurcation between
culture and nature used as the polar situation of myth by
Lévi-Strauss. Vidal-Naquet understands hunting to be the
deciding additional factor in the relationship between culture
and nature. The human hunt entailed the use of technology to
assert the dominance of the hunter (see chapter eight). This
skill, encouraged by some of the ephebeian rites, was useful in
the wilds to survive by finding foods and also to set ambushes
to capture the enemy in night patrols. The same skill proved
useful in the political life of the city, where, as Vidal-Naquet
discusses, the Greek male asserted his dominance. The ephebe
promised to continue that tradition when "he guarantees in his
hoplite oath to protect the boundary stones of his country
...."[49] Those boundary stones marked not only the
geographical limits but also the symbolic limits for the
demarcation of political and ideological power.
    Vidal-Naquet has dedicated himself to defining the
political and ideological limits of culture through myth. For
him, the Sophoclean presentation of Oedipus was "designed as
part of an ongoing aesthetic, ideological and cultural
debate."[50] That "debate" is encoded by myth. The historian's
task is to decode the myth by revealing the frontiers beneath
the fact that "fables take different shapes in Argos, in Athens,
in Sparta."[51] Some of those changes in form can be explained
by the political reality of each community.
    Vidal-Naquet seeks to "rediscover the facts beneath the
words, the reality beneath the memories, the truth beneath the

lies or the fabrication."[52] By separating these out, he not only fulfills his calling as a historian but also assumes the role of a traitor. Vidal-Naquet encourages us to be vigilant against "mythologization." From Thucydides, who aimed at exactness in his accounts of the Peloponnesian War, Vidal-Naquet learned that words must change along with the events of war to demonstrate that the attributes of speakers change along with their discourse. Nicole Loraux, the fourth leader of the Gernet Center, takes issue with this agenda for the makers of myths. She claims that "Thucydides is not my colleague." Let us look at why she claims another heritage.

NOTES

1. Pierre Vidal-Naquet, *The Black Hunter*, tr. Andrew Szegedy-Maszak (Baltimore: Johns Hopkins University Press, 1986), p. xix.

2. Pierre Vidal-Naquet, "De l'erreur judiciaire au crime judiciaire," Afterword to Gisèle Tichané, *Coupable à tout prix—L'Affaire Luc Tangorre* (Paris: La Découverte, 1984), p. 193.

3. Nicole Loraux calls Vernant and Vidal-Naquet's *Mythe et tragédie en Grèce ancienne* the case for the "socio-archaeological context" of the communication between author and the audience of the fifth century B.C.: see her "L'Interférence tragique," *Critique*, XXIX, 317 (October 1973), p. 923.

4. In an interview with me in Paris on July 7, 1989 Vidal-Naquet used this word *polichilia* to describe his multifaceted pursuit of historical accuracy in the face of myths.

5. Vidal-Naquet, cited in Pierre Pachet, "Pierre Vidal-Naquet," *Critique*, XXXVIII, 418 (March 1982), p. 216.

6. Pierre Vidal-Naquet, *Les Juifs: la mémoire et le présent* (Paris: Maspero, 1981), p. 81.

7. Pierre Vidal-Naquet, "Oedipus in Vicenza and in Paris: Two Turning Points in the History of Oedipus," in his and Vernant's *Myth and Tragedy in Ancient Greece*, tr. Janet Lloyd (New York: Zone, 1988), p. 362.

8. This quotation is taken from Jean Jaurès (1859-1914) during his defense of Alfred Dreyfus. It is reprinted in Pierre Vidal-Naquet, *L'Affaire Audin* (Paris: Minuit, 1958).

9. Pierre Vidal-Naquet, "De l'erreur judiciaire," p. 194.

10. Bernard Knox, "Greece à la française," *The New York Review of Books* (March 3, 1983), p. 30. Knox mistakenly refers to an important article by Pierre Pachet on Vidal-Naquet's life and work as having appeared in the March 1982 issue of *Esprit*. The correct journal is *Critique*.

11. Pierre Vidal-Naquet and Jacques Le Goff, "Lévi-Strauss en Brocéliande," in Raymond Bellour and Catherine Clément, eds., *Claude Lévi-Strauss* (Paris: Gallimard, 1979), p. 274.

12. Loraux, "L'Interférence tragique," p. 924, discusses "confrontation" as appropriate to both Vernant and Vidal-Naquet. The term better describes Vidal-Naquet's work than Vernant's.

13. Pierre Vidal-Naquet, "Plato's Myth of the Statesman: The Ambiguities of the Golden Age and of History," tr. Maria Jolas, *Journal of Hellenic Studies*, XCVIII (1978), p. 132.

14. Pierre Vidal-Naquet speaks of "declaring war against this interpretation and depriving judeo-christian thought of the honor of having defined the historicity of humanity" (My translation of "Temps des dieux et temps des hommes," *Revue de l'histoire des religions*, CLVII [January 1960], p. 55).

15. Vidal-Naquet, "Land and Sacrifice in the *Odyssey*," in R. L. Gordon, ed., *Myth Religion and Society* (Cambridge: Cambridge University Press, 1981), p. 85.

16. Vidal-Naquet, *The Black Hunter*, p. xix.

17. Pierre Vidal-Naquet, "Oedipus in Athens," in his and Vernant's *Myth and Tragedy in Ancient Greece*, p. 307.

18. These essays are entitled "Oedipe à Athènes," "Oedipe entre deux cités," and "Oedipe à Vicence et à Paris." Vidal-Naquet and Vernant have collected essays on Oedipus in their *Oedipe et ses mythes* (Paris: Editions Complexe, 1988).

19. Vidal Naquet, "Oedipus in Athens," p. 319.

20. Pierre Vidal-Naquet, "Oedipus between Two Cities: An Essay on *Oedipus at Colonus*," in his and Vernant's *Myth and Tragedy in Ancient Greece*, p. 356.

21. Pierre Vidal-Naquet, "The Black Hunter Revisited," *Proceedings of the Cambridge Philological Society*, XXXII (1986), p. 135.

22. Vidal-Naquet, "Oedipus between Two Cities," p. 339.

23. Vidal-Naquet, *The Black Hunter*, p. 107.

24. Vidal-Naquet, "Oedipus in Athens," pp. 311-2.

25. *Ibid.*, p. 311.

26. Vidal-Naquet, "Oedipus between Two Cities," p. 353.

27. *Ibid.*, p. 355.

28. Pierre Vidal-Naquet, "Oedipus in Vicenza and in Paris," in his and Vernant's *Myth and Tragedy in Ancient Greece*, p. 375.

29. Pierre Vidal-Naquet, in his and Alain Schnapp's *Journal de la Commune Etudiante* (Paris: Seuil, 1969), p. 8.

30. *Ibid.*, p. 51.

31. Vidal-Naquet, *Les Juifs*, p. 11.

32. Cited in Pachet, p. 216.

33. Vidal-Naquet, "De l'erreur judiciaire," p. 195.

34. Pierre Vidal-Naquet, *Torture: The Cancer of Democracy* (Baltimore: Penguin, 1963), p. 167.

35. Pierre Vidal-Naquet, "Slavery and the Rule of Women in Tradition, Myth, and Utopia," in *Myth, Religion and Society*, pp. 193ff.

36. *Ibid.*, p. 198.

37. Vidal-Naquet, *The Black Hunter*, p. 209.

38. Vidal-Naquet, in his and M. M. Austin's *Economic and Social History of Ancient Greece*, tr. M. M. Austin (Berkeley: University of California Press, 1977), p. 166 n. 8.

39. Vidal-Naquet, *The Black Hunter*, p. 5.

40. Pierre Vidal-Naquet and Pierre Lévêque, *Clisthène l'Athénien* (Paris: Les Belles Lettres, 1964), p. 77.

41. Vidal-Naquet, "The Black Hunter Revisited," pp. 126-27.

42. The work of Vidal-Naquet has been translated into Italian and has been generally well received. One exception is Vincenzo Di Benedetto, who, along with Alessandro Lami, has accused Vidal-Naquet, Vernant, Detienne, and Moses Finley of being "mystifying" scholars. See Di Benedetto and Lami's *Filologia e marxismo: Contro le mistificazioni* (Naples: Liguori, 1980).

43. Knox, "Greece à la française," p. 30.

44. Pierre Vidal-Naquet, "La Tradition de l'hoplite athénien," in Jean-Pierre Vernant, ed., *Problèmes de la guerre en Grèce Ancienne* (Paris: Ecole des hautes études en sciences sociales, 1985), p. 166.

45. Vidal-Naquet, "The Black Hunter Revisited," p. 134.

46. See chapter eight of this book and Françoise Frontisi-Ducroux's *Dédale, mythologogie de l'artisan* (Paris: Maspero, 1975).

47. Pierre Vidal-Naquet, "Bêtes, hommes et dieux chez les Grecs," in Leon Poliakov, ed., *Hommes et Bêtes: Entretiens sur le racisme* (Paris: Mouton, 1975), p. 134.

48. *Ibid.*, p. 133.

49. Pierre Vidal-Naquet, "The Black Hunter and the Origin of the Athenian *ephebeia*," in *Myth, Religion and History*, p. 162.

50. Pierre Vidal-Naquet, "Oedipus in Vicenza and in Paris," in his and Vernant's *Myth and Tragedy in Ancient Greece*, p. 374.

51. Vidal-Naquet, *The Black Hunter*, p. xxiii.

52. Vidal-Naquet, *Les Juifs*, p. 11.

53. Pierre Vidal-Naquet, "Platon, L'Histoire et les historiens," in Jacques Brunschwig, ed., *Histoire et structure* (Paris: Vrin, 1985), p. 157.

Chapter Seven

LORAUX: THE MYTHS OF DEATH AND LIFE

Thucydides is universally acknowledged as the founder of historiography, the science of history. At the same time, Herodotus is known as the father of history. The two writers present two clearly distinct attitudes about history. Herodotus entertains his reader with anecdotes that focus upon a story to the detriment of factual documentation. Thucydides, by contrast, aims at exactness by including the texts of speeches for example, relies more on description, and analyzes history by attributing causes to events. Scientifically minded historians have preferred the more empirically concerned Thucydides.

Nicole Loraux is skeptical about the scientific reliability of Thucydides. She describes the goal of Thucydides as "writing a text which makes us forget that it is a text, which introduces itself as a privileged document, an open window on Greek reality, and at the same time closes this reality like the reality of the text by setting up before the already conquered reader a discursive monument."[1] Although Thucydides claims to be writing a "treasure" to last through the ages, his writings, like many other ancient texts, must be understood as "functioning at once as sources of information on day-to-day social living," not just as "classics of Greek literature."[2] In Thucydides' text there are gaps, silences, and omissions which he did not intend as the writer of a historical document. As Loraux points out, the ancient writer and the contemporary reader thus understand history in different ways. The scientific method Thucydides intended breaks down under the scrutiny of specialists of narrative called narratologists. Loraux is one of these narratologists as she analyzes "the discursive

monument" of historical documents. In the intersection of
history and literature she discovers a strategy of reading to
help avoid the authoritative, transparent role given to
historiography. Let us look at who this narratologist is.

Trained as a classicist, Loraux also utilizes history,
psychology, and sociology. In the afterword to one of her
articles she is described as a "sociologist of ancient Greece."[3]
Loraux certainly displays her breadth of knowledge across the
social sciences in her pursuit of the myths of death among the
Greeks. Her dissertation was about the uniqueness of the
Athenian tradition of giving funeral orations on the occasion
of a soldier's death in battle. It was published in 1981 as
L'Invention d'Athènes (*The Invention of Athens*, 1986). That
same year she also published a study of why Athenians were
named after the goddess Athena (*Les Enfants d'Athéna*). In
1985 her *Façons tragiques de tuer une femme* (translated in
1987 as *Tragic Ways of Killing a Woman*) presented the kinds
of deaths attributed to women by Greek tragedies. She has also
published many articles on what the Greek myths of death
have to say about the roles played by the surviving Greek men
and women. Her research elaborates the studies of women by
Vernant, Detienne, and Vidal-Naquet.

Loraux adapts some of the structuralist ideas of Lévi-
Strauss. She applies his concepts of autochthony ("born of the
earth"), homology (the system of a set of symbolic values), and
totemism to the "ethnographical context" of fourth- and fifth-
century Greece. For example, the first Athenian is reputed to
have been Erichthonios, who was born of the earth.
Autochthony thus becomes "the essence of all the citizens (a
men's only club) ... whereby the intervention of the fertile
earth comes to solace the refusal of sexual union."[4] Gender
differentiation in Athens derives from this myth of Athenian
origin. Loraux thus applies the Lévi-Straussian categories to
the cultural milieu of Greek myths and thereby analyzes the
social value of gender roles in Greek society.

Loraux's analysis of Greek funeral orations seeks to
"undermine any notion we may have had of an Athens always
homogeneous to itself."[5] Instead, she proposes that Athenians
were hypnotized into accepting competing myths about their

social roles and their relationships to one another. Her insights emanate from the observation that "the orators hypnotize men's souls by celebrating the city and by confusing life and death, past and present, in an amalgam from which the living alone benefit."[6] There were gaps between *logos* and *ergon* (action) in fourth- and fifth-century Athens. What was being said in the rhetorical speeches and documents recorded by historians like Thucydides was not consistent with how people were conducting themselves. Hence Nicole Loraux embarks upon "the reading of a text ... nourished by a constant interaction between its contents and its context ... some mythical totality we call Greek culture."[7] Here we see her argument about a contextual method to expose Greek culture itself as a myth.

Loraux's strategy has been to interweave history with psychology in order to present the place of myth in the course of history. She brings together the Greek city-states and myths, not to reduce either one to the other but to show how they have influenced each other. Her "desire to place myth within the confines of the city-state"[8] is a reaction to the French university, where myth is a disparaged term.

Loraux has established herself as an authority on the presence of myth as a historically valid component built into the very method of doing research into the past. For example, she presents tragedy as a product of the "perpetual interchange between myth and the city-state, a ceaseless swing of the pendulum between the *polis* [the city] and the *épos* [the story]."[9] The swinging pendulum upon which tragedy was constructed also provided many other ethical byproducts in the daily lives of Greeks. The story of the "glorious death" of a soldier in battle had ramifications for men and women in both Sparta and Athens, where it was customary to give funeral orations for fallen heroes. The stories determined what it meant to be honorable. These stories were told by orators using a hypnotic rhetoric analyzed by Loraux. Her insights into myth reveal the twisted social life of Athens and the values of the Greeks disguised in its rhetoric.

ATHENS AS THE CIVILIZED *POLIS*

Autochthony, the birth of humanity from the earth rather than from women, is part of the unique beginnings that Athenians attributed to themselves. The womenless origins of Athenian men provide a mythical basis for a city characterized as a place where "*logos* is to be found entirely."[10] The *logos* had an especially strong presence in reaffirming the myth of the "beautiful death" of a soldier in battle through the use of funeral orations delivered by men about men. Both *muthos* and *logos* thus seem to ignore the presence of women in Athenian society.

Loraux goes beyond those appearances to discern a difference between what is said and what is happening. Like Jacques Derrida's "deconstruction," which focuses on artificially composed dualities to demonstrate their flowing into each other, Loraux's method "deconstructs" the apparent absence of Athenian women to reveal their presence as listeners to the funeral orations and also as subjects about whom much is said. Women are both the survivors of the martyred soldiers and those who listen to the epic tales of battle being narrated to give present meaning to their soldier's absence. The presence of these women exemplifies what Loraux calls "the divergence between civic thought and epic formulation."[11] That "divergence" is especially reflected in the way in which Greek law creates a fictive representation of reality—as if to coerce people into behaving in ways other than the ways in which they would do without these models.

The Periclean law on bilateral kinship exemplifies this divergence between *logos* and *ergon*. While Pericles (c. 495-429 B.C.) decreed a law specifying that kinship would be determined by both father and mother, the daily lives of Athenians were wrought with examples of the prejudicial preferences implied by the acceptance of autochthonous origins. Loraux remarks that the autochthonous myth ran contrary to the Periclean law by projecting "the desire to deny the reality of reproduction by a society of men, whose experience was that those things that matter were passed on among men."[12] In fact, kinship, parenthood, and progeny were not equally attributed to men and women. As we shall discuss, Loraux argues that the priority of the public realm over the private in Athenian society produced a rhetorical and ideological reality that masked a dualistic world. The word (*logos*) and everyday life (*ergon*) split to reveal women with values and privileges independent and often counter to those given to them in myths.

Loraux's study of the funeral orations in Athens examines the differences between the private and the public lives of Athenians. The democratic ideals of Athens gave all its citizens the same honors. The most personal and private event of death became a public event upon the "beautiful death" of a warrior. Since Athens inverted the order of other Greek cities by making citizenship prerequisite for the hoplite soldier (in a law known as the "hoplite reform"), the Athenian warrior's death received the acknowledgment of the community with an oration delivered in honor of the individual's sacrifice on behalf of the community. The collective, or public, nature of this "beautiful death" was emphasized. As opposed to the epic funerals, in which an individual soldier's death was honored by his own funeral pyre or given a special sendoff on a ship or other individualized odyssey, Athens utilized collective funerals, grave markers, and funeral orations to commemorate the "beautiful deaths" of the warriors killed in battle. Loraux recalls Vernant's insight that the funeral pyre was a reverse of the sacrificial offering in that only white bones remained from the pyre while in the sacrifice bones went up in smoke to the gods and the meat was eaten by humans. The reversal is significant because of the special, mythological significance of the "beautiful death" of the warrior.

Loraux's analyses explain why this death was rendered "mythological." For her, mythological means rhetorical. In Athens, for example, the funeral orations gave value to military death by bestowing civic honor on an event presented as the supreme achievement of manly excellence (*arete*). These orations thus create the myth of "beautiful death" for Athenians. The orations became opportunities to compose ideologies for the city, to narrate a commonweal out of the event of death. Loraux points out that the occasion was timely for the verbal development of the collective good. Her analyses of the orations demonstrate that "*the beautiful death is already discourse by its very nature*: a rhetorical trope, the privileged locus for the rooting of an ideology from the world of Achilles to that of the democratic city-state."[13] The words invent a myth out of the reality of death. The myth is a civic one because the glory of Athens the city-state is promulgated on the occasion of the deaths of its military heroes. This "civilized" approach to the horror of death is also a commentary on life because the orations were delivered to the survivors. The delivery was a special occasion for recalling a host of values upon which the warrior's death as "beautiful" was parasitic.

THE CITY "WITHOUT GENDER"

According to Loraux, the funeral oration was a hypnotic form of *logos*. The words of the rhetorician constituted "a piece of sorcery *(goeteia)*, that is, deception."[14] The "sorcery" entailed the hypnotic mix of military, civic, and male values in the Athenian way of life. The deception was brought about through the ideological misrepresentation of Athens as a "city without gender"—its women playing no distinctive roles. In such a city autochthony served as "an etiological myth for this exclusion of women."[15] Autochthony thus gave an originating cause—i.e. "etiological myth"—for not differentiating men and women since in these myths women have nothing to do with the birth of humanity. Likewise women did not play a role in the "glorious death" intended for males by males. Hence the funeral oration perpetuated women's insignificance by addressing them as the recipients of the male messages about birth and death.

The military role for Athenian men was especially assigned by the "hoplitic reforms" of the later fifth century. Hoplites were the heavily armed infantry soldiers of the Greek city-states. As Loraux observes, in Athens hoplites had to be citizens, thus inverting the order of the other Greek cities. As citizens, they thus already owned full membership in Athenian society rather than had to earn it by distinguished military service. The Athenian hoplites could then concentrate on distinguishing themselves militarily for which they would receive social honors. As hoplites, they provided their own armor and so contributed personally to the military budget of the Athenian community. They thus already had a stake in the military prior to their actual service. Within that system the "glorious death" of the warrior in battle is described by Loraux as part of a "paradigm"[16] of values easily assimilated by the individual hoplite as part of his communal life.

The Athenian funeral oration canonized those who realized that most honored of military values by attributing to them the posthumous title of "stout-hearted men." Once again, the *logos* precluded women from this noble form of death. Women listened to the funeral orations, citing the glory of their fallen men, or waited for life to resume upon the return of their fathers, brothers, uncles, or male cousins. As listeners, they were the receivers of the messages that death in war made men aristocratic in the glory they officially received. Although the funerals and the tombs were collective experiences because of the egalitarian city-state,[17] a man's glory was carried forward individually in the funeral orations delivered on his behalf. As Loraux points out, "the city ... had no comment to make on a woman's death."[18]

THE MONSTROUS AMAZONS

A woman who died in childbirth was given special status. In Sparta, a woman who died in childbirth had the same right as a male killed in combat to have her name etched on a tombstone. Loraux studies this link ("Le Lit, La Guerre" [the bed and the war]) between the men and women. Although Spartans did not have funeral orations, the engraved tombstones were the Spartan *logos* in the service of rendering glory to human efforts. A woman dying in the throes of her combat with life was remembered along with men who died as hoplites. A woman who died in childbirth gave testimony to what Loraux calls "birth as the test of virility."[19] Conversely, the mythical Hercules (Herakles) was also more virile because he assumed feminine traits. He was the incarnation of so many male virtues that the excess had to be made believable. Some Greek myths thus portrayed Hercules as wearing women's clothes, taking hot baths, and assuming feminine behavior from time to time.[20] Women's behavior was therefore sometimes acknowledged by male society.

The reality of daily life for the Greek woman was, however, usually more dreary. Her work was restricted to the home, where she was out of sight of the men's workplace, and she was never to be found legitimately in the warriors' midst. There were exceptions—above all, the Amazon women who lived on the fringes of the known world. Whether or not Amazons really existed, they represent women who defeated men at the masculine game of war by being women in body and men in soul.[21] The Amazons were thereby characterized as monsters, for they neither resided by the family hearth nor were submissive.The "monstrous" Amazons provided a striking contrast to Athenian women.

According to Loraux, the difference between Athena, the goddess after whom Athens was named, and Athenian women is also telling. Athena is not the mother of Athenians. Athenian men were originally born of the earth. However, there is no original Athenian mother for men. Athenian women constitute a tribe unto themselves and part of what Loraux calls the "race of women,"[22] descended from Pandora, that first Greek woman created from glaze (rather than germinated in the earth, as was man) and given to man as a retribution for his having tricked the gods. By this event "the introduction of women into the world separated men from the gods." [23]

The namesake of Athens, Athena, is a virgin usually portrayed fully armed in her role as a warrior goddess. Loraux observes that "Athena is not comical by contrast with a woman in her home who prepares to don her helmet and lance to attack her husband."[24] Athena is also the goddess of wisdom. Athenian women looked at statues of Athena dressed in the military model of virtue. It is as if men created Athena in their likeness and suited to their own fantasies. Athena offers contradictory messages for the women of Athens. Athena is not married, nor is she a mother. The typical fate of women in Athens was very different.

Nicole Loraux seeks more information about the question of the woman in Athens. The Athenian woman was not a citizen. She had no right to vote. There is no word for an Athenian woman in Greek. On the one hand, she was not a part of the *logos*. On the other hand, she was immersed in the daily work (*ergon*) and commerce of men desirous of a family and a hearth. The autochthonous origins of Athenian men served to deny another reality of the distinctive condition of women: the bearing of children. Loraux explores this dissociation of sensibility between the *logos* and the *ergon* to probe the myth of autochthony introduced into the Oedipus myth by Lévi-Strauss. The imaginary or fantastic basis for the myth rests upon "the desire of a society of men, whose experience is that what matters is passed among men, to deny the reality of reproduction."[25] The effect is to cause women to disappear.

The stage became a safe place for the expression of the fictional existence of women in Athens. Since a woman often did not have the same intellectual or political reality as a man, her choices were also voiced differently. Loraux argues that Greek tragedy was an especially revealing medium because the "stage [was] set up by the city for the tangling and untangling of actions that anywhere else it would be dangerous or intolerable even to think about."[26] In tragedies women hung themselves. The rope and the neck were women's ignominious alternatives to the sword and the breast used in the suicides of men as signs of socially approved courage (*andreia*). According to Loraux, suicide was "a woman's solution."[27] She did not belong anyway, so that to terminate her own life was consistent with her absent status. Invariably, Greek tragedy also portrays women as dying in their beds. The place for the realization of their sexual lives as lovers and mothers is thus also their identity.

Vernant, Detienne, and Vidal-Naquet all comment upon the exclusion of women as a founding principle of Athens.

Loraux's contribution is to explore the psychological bases for the exclusions. She contends that misogyny is an "over-facile notion."[28] The suffering of women in the birth of children was simply outside male experience. The "beautiful death" of the warrior in battle was likewise denied to the female Greek. Men controlled the words while women were expected to be silent and to listen.

SILENCE AS THE ADORNMENT OF WOMEN

The ultimate silence of women—their death—was an especially unheralded event for the Athenians. When, however, a woman adopted what Loraux calls "the feminine way of dying"[29]—suicide by hanging—a woman gained more attention because she employed a way out which for a man would have been humiliating. Men were expected to seek the "beautiful death" in combat. The noose became a woman's way to reject her fate within this life by assuming control over her life with a weapon that was all her own.

A Greek woman's ordinary glory was to avoid being talked about at all:

> It was in the depths of her house that a Greek woman
> was supposed to live out her existence as young girl,
> as wife, and as mother; and it was shut up in her
> house, far from the gaze of others, that she had to end
> her life.[30]

In Greek tragedy, however, woman secured a special audience. She acted in an uncommon way because the stage gave her a chance for glory: suicide *by hanging*. Vernant and Detienne (*Cunning Intelligence in Greek Culture and Society*) establish that the noose was representative of cunning intelligence (*mètis*) in that the rope and the noose were devices to trap animals or humans. As the vehicle for a woman's suicide, the rope likewise was a means for a woman to gain authority over her life by inventing a death uniquely her own. Blood was a sign of a noble death for men and the healthy functioning of life for women: "the natural flow of blood which ensured the good functioning of women's bodies was placed on the same plane as the open wound in the virile body."[31] Blood as the sign of life was given symbolic sanction as the life of society even though blood was literally associated with the violent death of men. In death, Greek women could not identify themselves with blood. This was already chosen as men's source of nobility. On stage women chose their own form of death, in which ironically no blood flowed.

Of course, the choking resulting from hanging was also consistent for a Greek woman whose life was supposed to be devoted to silence. In a society in which a woman's voice was not publicly sanctioned—for she could not deliver a public oration either in a democratic forum or on the occasion of a funeral—we see one of the first instances of "silence ... [as] the adornment of women"[32] in the city-state in which men controlled the *logos*. The Spartans allowed the names of women who died in childbirth to be engraved on tombstones alongside the names of the male warriors who had fallen in combat. Thus in Sparta the silence of maternity became a way for a woman to test the mettle of her "virile worth"[33] in childbirth. The painful throes of childbirth and the combat of war thus became synonymous means to achieve glory for both women and men.

Nevertheless, the majority of Greek women belonged to their own community or "race." Greek mythology portrays Pandora as the first in the "race of women." Hesiod's *Theogony* (c. 670 B.C.) presents her not as the mother of humanity but rather as the mother of women. Her origins as artifice and as a scourge to mankind set up the gulf between the genders.

However, the gulf was not always so wide. Loraux finds a dialectical blending of male and female ideals in the most apparently virile of stereotypes: Hercules. Although he is typically remembered for his masculine feats of strength and endurance, Hercules also enjoys women's luxuries of warm baths and feminine garments. Loraux reminds us that this blend of male and female traits also resides in Hera who possesses the ambivalence of virile strength as a goddess of war and the cunning intelligence of a spouse able to reveal the infidelities of her husband.[34] Social and political misogyny thus did not preclude either admiration for certain "feminine" virtues in men or the adoption of "masculine" behavior by women.

The coexistence of masculine with feminine virtues in Greek mythological figures tells us that women spoke despite their public silence. The Greeks thus did not believe that either the masculine or the feminine contained all truth. Loraux imagines a "dialectic"—better, dialogue—between one side and the other. Like Detienne, Loraux herself often uses the Socratic maieutic to engage her reader in her work. Her questions are not rhetorical. Instead, questions are the point of departure for developing a dialogical style.

The Greek struggle between *logos* and *ergon* can be understood as the dialogical motor of change for the masculine and feminine codes. The glory of a "beautiful death" for the warrior was the subject of many a funeral oration. Meanwhile a woman struggled through childbirth without any personal glory except in Sparta, where her mortal silence gave her an engraving on a tombstone. Both of these struggles involved the essence of manhood and womanhood—the one in mortal combat and the other in childbirth.

Loraux remarks that the liver is a crucial organ for the death blow in combat. Likewise Greek medical studies indicate that the liver protects the infant in the womb but will also result in the mother's death if it is struck during childbirth.[35] The same biological organ leads to glory for both men and women in their struggles for survival on their mutually exclusive battlefields. The unity of that biological destiny was especially recognized in the Oedipus myth, whose women Loraux credits with insights into the psychological dimensions of this story for the Greeks and all of humanity.

OEDIPAL WOMEN IN SEARCH OF THEMSELVES

In the words of the Oedipus myth Nicole Loraux finds some resolution of the gap between the Greek *logos*, which ascribes civic death for women, and the *ergon*, in which women are inscribed in the daily lives of the Greeks. Her reading of the Oedipus myth endows its four principal feminine figures with a life that provides an alternative to what she calls "the sterile opposition between feminism and misogyny."[36] Loraux offers a psychological reading of the tragic context that has been "masked" (to use Vernant's description of the situation prior to Loraux)[37] by the labeling of the Greeks as misogynistic. The Sphinx, Merope, Antigone, and Jocasta provide crucial examples of the struggles of Greek women.

Loraux adapts the structuralism of Lévi-Strauss to help understand how the Sphinx, Merope, and Antigone are crucial women in Oedipus' odyssey from young warrior to defeated elderly man. Totemism, autochthony, and homology are the key concepts in Loraux's adaptation of the Lévi-Strauss scheme to a contextualist reading of the Oedipus story.

The principle of totemism—the worship of an animal or natural object as the blood origin of a clan—is used by Loraux to speak about the distinctively female soul and race ascribed to women by Greek writers. Pandora, as a created being—a natural object made of clay—is the totemic model for the challenge represented in women for men. The totem is Pandora's chest, which contains the sources of human pain for men. However, that object has become an objective correlative for the naive association of human scourges and danger with women. In the myth of Oedipus alternative models offer complex and credible examples of women working within a social system in which the principles of totemism, autochthony, and homology influence conceptions about women. The totem provided a simple model to which misogynists of the day could refer.

In her recent research[38] the classicist Mary Lefkowitz maintains that intelligence rather than beauty or sexuality made women at once appealing and dangerous to the Greeks. The Sphinx is thus sent by Hera to Thebes as the ultimate female challenge to male self-knowledge. Although the Sphinx is a monster, she, the incarnation of intellectual prowess, is clearly female because the parameters of her riddle cannot be identified as clearly as those of Pandora's box. She asks the Thebans the riddle about the three ages of manhood. When they are unable to answer her correctly, she devours a Theban, including Haemon, the son of Jocasta's brother, Creon. As the supreme female capable of confounding the intelligence of men and thus menacing their identity, the Sphinx represents the crafty, reflective side of human nature (*mètis*). Oedipus has to master this skill on his way toward maturity once he declares his independence by killing Laius. The Sphinx becomes a threat to the life of Thebes. By solving the riddle of the Sphinx, Oedipus is victorious over a totem and also reincorporates the female *mètis* into his own being. Mètis is a goddess devoured by Zeus in his attempt to incorporate male and female virtue. Likewise Oedipus appropriates craftiness into his male being and receives the acknowledgment of the Thebans by being made their king.

The Sphinx is silenced by the intelligent resolution of her riddle by Oedipus. Loraux postulates silence as the adornment of women in Greek politics. Their word was not welcome in the civic forum since they were not citizens. This silence also goes back to Pandora, who was given to mankind as a curse by Zeus. Whereas Athenian men took pride in their earth-born (autochthonous) nature, they relegated women to silence as part of this myth of human origins. Loraux points out that Hesiod's *Theogony* portrays the first woman as not being deceitful because there was nothing beneath the appearances.[39] In other words, woman has no substance. And so it is with Merope, the woman who became the mother of Oedipus while he was growing up in Corinth. Silence is her lot. We know little about her except her name. She has no words to mask. Her reality is the daily struggle of raising a young boy. None of the Greek writers or commentators mentions her work. She is suddenly abandoned when Oedipus decides to consult the oracle of Apollo and then to flee Corinth. Merope is the incarnation of the Greek woman fastidiously going about her daily business without glory and in silence. Merope does that task so well that Oedipus mistakes her for his natural mother after consulting the oracle at Delphi. Her work is remembered not in words but in the action that Oedipus takes to head off toward Thebes. Merope is thus representative of the silent, self-effacing mother whose reality is in the work (*ergon*) rather than in the verbal (*logos*) perpetuation of glory.

By contrast with Merope, Antigone is a woman who, for Loraux, succeeds twice. Not only is she able to control her own life and death through her suicide, but she is also victorious over Creon by subjecting him to the ignominy he tries so hard to avoid. He cannot execute her by burying her alive. She takes that power away from him by hanging herself with her virgin's veil. Antigone thus represents a homology for women who succeed in Greek tragedy by finding a death all their own. Hanging is the death reserved for grieving wives. As the exemplary nurse dedicated to caring for her aging father, she also defends the honor of her brother Polynices, whose burial was forbidden by Creon as punishment for Polynices' disloyalty.

Antigone's life is, then, a dedication to the glory of the men in her family. She becomes a martyr to the very cause she dies rejecting: the family name. Vidal-Naquet characterizes that family as "the incestuous and monstrous family of Oedipus and the Labdacids."[40] Antigone is thus allied with a monstrous group. Meanwhile her sister, Ismene, who does nothing except keep the secret of Antigone's decision to oppose Creon's will, perpetuates the ideal of the loyal woman who preserves unity in the household.

Antigone's opposition to Creon demonstrates a courage socially unacceptable for woman. As Loraux puts it, "Women, of course, must not desert their nature by showing courage (*andreia*), and the Amazons are monstrous because they violated this rule."[41] The word for courage (*andreia*) is associated with men (*andres*). Antigone's courage is to refuse Creon's attempt to control her death as well as her life. She chooses the woman's way out: suicide by hanging. Loraux reminds us that the knotted veil used by Antigone to hang herself is also "one of the instruments of seduction."[42] Antigone the virgin thus takes control of her own sexuality by killing herself:

> Antigone, who dies for putting a dead brother before
> life as a spouse, was confronted in death with a
> marriage, whether she was expected to 'find a husband
> in Hades,' as Creon put it, or was promised directly to
> the lord of the dead.[43]

Antigone's marriage must take place in another world
because she is the incarnation of what Loraux calls "absolute
disorder": she is a man-woman. Her action in choosing this
other world as her own once again underscores the working
(*ergon*) rather than verbal (*logos*) identity of women on the
Greek tragic stage. Greek women choose a realm other than
that of words for their own because, as Loraux tells us, "there
are no words available to denote the glory of a woman that do
not belong to the language of male renown."[44]

As a mother, Jocasta has a realm for herself in which
men cannot enter. As we have seen, Loraux's research ties
together the realms of the battlefield and the maternal bed as
the respective touchstones of male and female virtue. Female
virtue is defined by the negation of the male virtue of courage
and results in "not speaking of oneself."[45] This silence about
the self, so peculiar to Merope, also governs Jocasta's role as
mother of Oedipus. The act of choosing no longer to accept
this life and to choose the manner of exit for herself becomes
a critique against the silent life. Sophocles dramatizes such
breaks with silence as reflections upon Jocasta's unacceptable
acts as mother and as wife. Her choice of suicide is a decision
to exit with her identity as woman. She chooses hanging,
behind the closed doors of her marriage chamber, once again
modeling a woman's death. The spectator does not see Jocasta's
death, but rather the body of a dead woman. That dead body
is a commentary on the silence and inertness of her life. The
final act is not even worthy of being shown.

Jocasta's maternity is far more interesting than Sophocles
would have us understand. Loraux directs us to the Jocasta
depicted by Euripides in his *Phoenician Women*. There Jocasta
is, in Loraux's words, "exclusively a mother."[46] This Jocasta
chooses to die by the sword at the same place where her sons

Eteocles and Polynices died. She chooses the much feared death by the sword through the breast. Yet Jocasta's death is also that of a mother with her children, accepting their choice of death as hers. Loraux views this Jocasta as choosing to "die only as a mother."[47] Jocasta thus becomes a mythic model for a woman to choose her own arena for her glory within a male-dominated world.

Loraux's Jocasta exemplifies a model for the women discussed by the French psychoanalyst Julia Kristeva (b. 1941). Kristeva stipulates that women's distinctive arena is the semiotic, a psychic energy and communication originated by the mother with her child during pregnancy. This semiotic arena is represented by Kristeva as the *chora*. The term *chora* comes from Plato's *Timaeus*. Describing an indeterminate movement "analogous to vocal or kinetic rhythm"[48] between a mother and her child in the womb, the semiotic *chora* is later extended into the languages of madness, poetry, and the irrational through laughter, word games, and prosody. Because this semiotic, or language of communication, is pre-Oedipal, it allows a place for woman in human psychology.

The semiotic *chora* is also subversive of the dominant male-oriented values and keeps women in the margins of mainstream social determination. The model for women is, as for Loraux's Jocasta, a maternal one and does not allow for the additional man-woman intervention as exemplified by the other women in the Oedipus myth. Loraux's Jocasta appropriates men's values for herself and does not succeed in personally subverting the victimization of motherhood. However, Jocasta's spirit of compromising male values survives in Antigone, who succeeds doubly as a heroic woman even without the maternal role so necessary for the male emulation of woman.

Loraux's presentation of the women in the Oedipus myth offers a wide range of possibilities. The context of the Greek tragic stage provides an arena within which to explore the possibilities not available in the daily lives of Greek women.

At the same time Loraux's own exploration of a semiotic place for women inspires others within the Gernet Center to seek to reconstruct the attitudes behind ancient myths—

attitudes masked by the texts. Recall her comment on the work
of Thucydides:

> his project as a historian ...[was] to write a text which
> would make us forget that it is a text, which
> introduces itself as a privileged document, an open
> window on Greek reality, which at the same time
> closes access to this reality as well as the reality of the
> text by setting up in front of the already overwhelmed
> reader a monument of discourse.[49]

Let us now turn to scholars at the Gernet Center to see how
they continue the work of the "new historicism."

NOTES

1. Nicole Loraux, "Thucydide n'est pas un collègue,"
Quaderni di storia, XII (July-December 1980), p. 71.
Translations from this work are my own.

2. *Ibid.*, p. 65.

3. See Nicole Loraux, "Mourir devant Troie, tomber pour
Athènes: De la gloire du héros à l'idée de la cité," *Social
Science Information*, XVII, 6 (1978), 817. All selections from
this article are my own translation.

4. Nicole Loraux, *Les Enfants d'Athéna: idées athéniennes
sur la citoyenneté et la division des sexes* (Paris: La
Découverte, 1984), p. 12. All selections from this work are my
own translation.

5. Nicole Loraux, *The Invention of Athens: The Funeral
Oration in the Classical City*, tr. Alan Sheridan (Cambridge:
Harvard University Press, 1986), p. 338.

6. *Ibid.*, p. 268.

7. *Ibid.*, p. vii.

8. Loraux, *Les Enfants d'Athéna*, p. 11.

9. Nicole Loraux, "L'Interférence tragique," *Critique*, XXIX, 317 (October 1973), 909. My translation.

10. Loraux, *The Invention of Athens*, p. 147.

11. Nicole Loraux, "Deux versions de la mort du combattant athénien," *Ancient Society*, VI (1975), p. 25. My translation.

12. Loraux, *Les Enfants d'Athéna*, p. 21.

13. Loraux, "Mourir devant Troie," p. 806.

14. Loraux, *The Invention of Athens*, p. 264.

15. *Ibid.*, p. 284.

16. Loraux, "Mourir devant Troie," p. 802.

17. *Ibid.*, pp. 802ff.

18. Nicole Loraux, *Tragic Ways of Killing a Woman*, tr. Anthony Forster (Cambridge: Harvard University Press, 1987), p. 2.

19. Nicole Loraux, "Le Lit, la Guerre," *L'Homme*, XXI, 1 (1981), p. 51. All translations from this article are my own.

20. Nicole Loraux, " Héraklès: Le surmâle et le féminin," *Revue française de psychanalyse*, XLVI (1982), pp. 697-729.

21. Loraux, *The Invention of Athens*, pp. 147ff.

22. Nicole Loraux, "Sur la Race des Femmes et Quelques-Unes de ses Tribus," *Arethusa*, XI, 1-2 (1973), pp. 43-87.

23. Loraux, *Les Enfants d'Athéna*, p. 117.

24. *Ibid.*, p. 69.

25. *Ibid.*, p. 21.

26. Loraux, *Tragic Ways of Killing a Woman*, p. 33.

27. *Ibid.*, p. 8.

28. Loraux, Abstract to "Le Lit, La Guerre," p. 67. My translation.

29. Nicole Loraux, "Le Corps étranglé: quelques faits et beaucoup de représentations," in *Du Châtiment dans la cité*, no ed. (Rome: Ecole française de Rome, 1984), p. 224. All translations from this article are my own.

30. Loraux, *Tragic Ways of Killing a Woman*, p. ix.

31. Loraux, "Le Corps étranglé," p. 216.

32. Loraux, *Tragic Ways of Killing a Woman*, p. 21.

33. Loraux, "Le Lit, La Guerre," p. 51.

34. Loraux, "Héraklès," pp. 723ff.

35. Loraux, "Le Lit, La Guerre," p. 46.

36. Loraux, *Tragic Ways of Killing a Woman*, p. 62.

37. Jean-Pierre Vernant, Preface to Pierre Vidal-Naquet, *Oedipe et ses Mythes* (Paris: Complexe, 1988), p. ix.

38. See Mary K. Lefkowitz, *Women in Greek Myth* (Baltimore: Johns Hopkins University Press, 1986).

39. Loraux, "Sur la race des femmes," p. 49.

40. Pierre Vidal-Naquet, "Oedipus in Athens," in his and Jean-Pierre Vernant's *Myth and Tragedy in Ancient Greece*, tr. Janet Lloyd (Sussex: Harvester Press, 1981), p. 314.

41. Loraux, *The Invention of Athens*, p. 134.

42. Loraux, *Tragic Ways of Killing a Woman*, p. 10.

43. *Ibid.*, p. 38.

44. *Ibid.*, p. 48.

45. Loraux, *The Invention of Athens*, p. 147.

46. Loraux, *Tragic Ways of Killing a Woman*, p. 15.

47. *Ibid.*, p. 26.

48. Julia Kristeva, *Revolution in Poetic Language*, tr. Margaret Waller (New York: Columbia University Press, 1984), p. 26.

49. Loraux, "Thucydide n'est pas un collègue," p. 71.

Chapter Eight

GERNET'S LEGACY: A FRENCH NEW HISTORICISM

Louis Gernet's name has been given to the Center for the Comparative Research of Ancient Societies, now located in L'École des Hautes Études en Sciences Sociales (EHESS). Gernet's name also lives on through the work of Vernant, Detienne, Vidal-Naquet, and Loraux. Vernant and Detienne attended his lectures at the Ecole Pratique des Hautes Études and have passed on his influence to another generation now being influenced by the Gernet Center's sponsorship of scholarly studies on ancient societies. This second generation is associated with a movement in the United States called "New Historicism." François Hartog, a specialist in Herodotus, has had his work translated into English in a series of books published on "new historicism" and edited by Stephen Greenblatt. Greenblatt, an American scholar of the English Renaissance, gave the term currency in a program for "new historicism" articulated in a special issue of the journal *Genre* in 1982.[1]

New historicism is an American reaction to Lévi-Strauss and Michel Foucault. One of its aims is to incorporate structuralist methods with traditional literary history. This goal explains why the Americans are so attracted to the Gernet School, which they perceive to be a form of French New Historicism. The new historical approach is similar to the application of a grid to a literary text. The grid is composed of a horizontal axis, which represents the cultural context of a historicist approach and a vertical axis, which traces the structural implications of the text.

A specialist in philology, law, and economic and social history, Louis Gernet studied comparative philology at the Ecole Normale in Paris and went on to earn a degree in law. After spending much of his career at the University of Algiers teaching Greek prose composition and publishing articles in obscure journals, he returned to Paris at the age of sixty-five in 1948 to lecture on ancient Greek society in the Ecole Pratique des Hautes Études. He died in 1962 and was elected posthumously to the prestigious Collège de France, to which Jean-Pierre Vernant would also be elected in 1975.

During Gernet's tenure at the Ecole Pratique he applied his philological training to ancient Greek society. He gave myth and religion key roles in the expresssion of Greek genius. In 1948, Gernet defined the Greek imagination, in which "the essential feature of mythical thought is not only that it is accompanied by images but that the images constitute a necessary instrument of the thought itself."[2] This insight has led many scholars of the second generation of the Gernet Center to examine how Greek myths were represented on vases, in rituals, dances, and feasts. The representation of the myths in various media provides commentary on the influences that the myths had in the daily lives of the Greeks.

Gernet also concentrated on the cultural context of crucial words in myths—terms such as "justice," "right," "home," "demon," and "pariah." His isolation of the linguistic origins of these Greek words reveals other concepts from which the words are borrowed. He was thereby able to trace the evolution of the legal and economic concepts assumed in myths. His studies of the legends, rituals, and festivals surrounding myths also provide a richer understanding of the Greek society that practiced religion. His work grounds the Greek imagination in the legal and economic values of the culture.

For example, Gernet's analysis of the Oedipus myth focuses the legal context of the defeat of the Sphinx. According to Gernet, Oedipus obtained both Jocasta and Thebes as the fulfillment of a contract worked out by Creon for anyone who could defeat the Sphinx.[3] In addition, Gernet demonstrates that Greek law provides the ready-made model for a *pharmakos* (scapegoat), an identity given to Oedipus by a Greek audience. Gernet's sketches for the broad outlines of the legal setting of Oedipus are currently being developed by his disciples in the Center—for example, by Vernant and Detienne in their analysis of the concepts of *mètis* and *daîmon*.

The "second generation" of Gernet Center scholars, which stands on the shoulders of the first generation, added more dimensions to Gernet's legal and economic map of the Greek culture. Vernant, as the founder of the Center, is the primary inspiration for both generations. Detienne and Vidal-Naquet have directed theses and served on the theses committees of Loraux, François Hartog, Françoise Frontisi-Ducroux, Annie Schnapp-Gourbeillon, François Lissarrague, Laurence Kahn, among others. Vidal-Naquet also has guided the publication of books by Suzanne Saïd, Florence Dupont, and Jean-Louis Durand from his influential editorial positions with Maspero and other presses.

Can the second generation of the Gernet Center be called "new historicists"? Some discussion of "new historicism" itself is first necessary. There is some controversy as to whether "new historicism" or "cultural poetics" is the preferable term for the method being applied. A student in Stephen Greenblatt's class objected to the use of "new historicism" because the practitioners of this perspective were not based on Marx, who had sought a "new science" of history.[4] Because Greenblatt was not respecting Marx's precedent by using the Marxian method of dialectical materialism, the student objected to using the term "new historicism." In response, Greenblatt began advocating the use of "cultural poetics" as a more accurate characterization of the structuralist orientation based upon accurate historical information. This alternate label is also a way to portray the literary appropriation of what the cultural anthropologist Clifford Geertz calls "thick description,"[5] whereby culture is understood as a text to be interpreted. The historian Hayden White, who had been writing about the narratives of history for many years before the invention of the term "new historicism," sees the unity of this approach as a broad vision "to supplement prevailing formalist practices by extending attention to the historical contexts in which literary texts originate."[6]

White's insight is helpful in dicussing the orientation of the second generation of the Gernet Center as "new historicism." Theirs is a description of Greek culture "thick" with the approaches of French structuralists like Lévi-Strauss, Barthes, and Foucault on the one hand and respect for traditional classical scholarship on the other. Loraux's remark that Thucydides is not a colleague has become a rallying cry: as noted at the end of chapter six, Vidal-Naquet took Loraux's remark as a model for a new kind of history, in effect a new historicism. In *The Mirror of Herodotus* (1988), François Hartog uses Thucydides as one of the models for recasting the work of Herodotus, long acknowledged as the "father of history." Thucydides said that "without autopsy there can be no history."[7] This "autopsy" presumes the death of the subject and the presence of a former living body. Hartog and Suzanne Saïd subject Herodotus to such an autopsy. This autopsy of Herodotus exposes other subjects elaborated by second generation scholars in the Gernet Center: the writing of myth by Jesper Svenbro, Florence Dupont, and Alain Moreau; the eidetic, or visual, imagination of Greek myths by François Lissarrague, Françoise Frontisi-Ducroux, and Laurence Kahn; the Greek artisan as purveyor of mythology, as found in the presentations of Alain Schnapp, Frontisi-Ducroux, and Philippe Borgeaud; and the role of animals in the Greek mythological cosmology, as delineated by Annie Schnapp-Gourbeillon, Jean-Louis Durand, Saïd, and Frontisi-Ducroux. The views of this generation of scholars will now be discussed.

A REVISIONIST VIEW OF HERODOTUS

As a historian, Herodotus wanted to narrate what happened. However, Herodotus was also a mythologist. Anecdotes were at the heart of his writing. It is sometimes difficult to separate fact from fiction in the work of Herodotus. Like Hesiod, he was concerned with an evolving "family," not of the gods but of the Greeks themselves. Unlike Hesiod, he was content to rely on others for his stories. Herodotus cited Hesiod and Homer as he evaluated "great deeds in retrospect," whether or not performed by Greeks. His tolerance of others is noteworthy. While his anecdotal style is criticized by Thucydides and others as unscientific, it is especially appropriate for those "new historicists" concerned with "narratology"—the craft of telling a story.

Translation is at the heart of Herodotus' craft as a historian. In Herodotus' world oral testimony is the predominant means of transmitting information. François Hartog notes the technique of the "father of history": "Always it is a case of writing down something said, never of transcribing something written."[8] Thus Herodotus moves from one medium to another. He mesmerizes readers with his written text. He is not only a historian but also an artist. Voltaire sees *three* sides of Herodotus: a historian, a great artist, and a liar.

The third identity, that of a liar, is the area on which Hartog focuses. Translating is a kind of lying. Hartog invokes the famous formula *traduttore / traditore* (translator as traitor) to speak about the work of Herodotus. These "lies" are transformations and elaborations of events to entertain his reader. In his many travels Herodotus gathers information from "private persons" (*idiotes*) about the cultures preceding and surrounding the Greeks. He records stories about the nomadic Scythians, whose military strategy is not to engage in the fixed warfare preferred by the hoplites but to flee, retreat, and remain hidden to be able to wander once again. Nevertheless, this people places the god of war Arès on a pedestal in its religion. Herodotus portrays this myth of Arès as a fiction about their otherness to the Greeks: "the reason Arès can occupy the central position within Scythian space is that in Greece itself he is a marginal figure."[9] For Hartog, Herodotus thus develops a rhetoric of otherness which is naturally part of his task as a translator. In his respect for the otherness of cultures not his own, Herodotus must "lie" about the events of these cultures because he is translating the events into a foreign language and presenting them so that that foreign culture (his own) can understand them. Paradoxically, Herodotus never learns a foreign language.

The Amazons are another example of a story about otherness originally reported by Herodotus. According to Hartog, Thucydides accuses Herodotus of gullibility in literally taking information that becomes part of his mythology: "He [Herodotus] believed when he should not have (unconscious liar); he pretended to believe when he should not have (liar, pure and simple)."[10] And yet the "lies" of Herodotus are taken by Hartog to be more truthful than Thucydides realizes. The implied message of Herodotus is, as Hartog presents it, that "saying is as good as seeing." The validity of the "sayings" in Herodotus is reenacted during the Hellenistic period when, as Hartog notes, the authors of romances cite Herodotus to give their texts the impression of reality.

In a "structural" reading of Herodotus, Suzanne Saïd and Michèle Rosellini survey Herodotus' description of how "savage" women and men exchange gender roles. The Amazons are only one example of role reversal. The Zaueces and the Auses are other tribes in which martial skills among women are respected and displayed in community festivals. Conversely, Herodotus offers examples of men who adopt maternal roles. For example, he notes the existence of "the community of women"[11] among both the Scythians and the Massagetes and also reports the differences in sexual mores. Women's sexual prowess is a determining factor for tribes such as the Gindanes, who esteem a woman for the number of lovers she has, and the nomadic Libyans, who practice an institutionalized polygamy. For Herodotus, these mores offer an inviting contrast to the Greeks, who criticize Helen of Troy for not conforming to their own ethic of monogamy. Likewise the Greeks are highly critical of spouses who wear makeup and perfume. The place of women in Greek society is defined precisely, but in the so-called "savage" societies women have more choices.

Yet Herodotus did not simply present a series of role reversals between men and women. Rather he represented the situation of Greek gender as a reaction to the otherness of the surrounding peoples. As Saïd and Rosellini put it:

> Although Herodotus' story juxtaposes in a given universe people characterized by the virility of their women or by the effeminate conduct of their men, at no moment does he effectively make them complements of each another nor does he portray a society wherein women would be completely substituted for men.[12]

Saïd and Rosellini are not members of the Gernet Center even though they presented this study there. Influenced especially by Vernant and Vidal-Naquet, they title their work "structural." They are in the spirit of what Loraux has been developing: focusing upon the otherness of Greek women within classical myths.

Meanwhile, the focus upon Herodotus opens the possibility of a "French new historicism" for second generation scholars. Gernet's concerns with origins in his tracing of etymons are ever-present. The subject of history is the touchstone for revealing problems in the communication of myths among the Greeks. Hartog reveals, for example, that, although Herodotus' history is written for posterity to read, the world of Herodotus is to be understood "not as a world of writing."[13] And so the history of myth provides the opportunity to examine the parameters for writing and non-writing as these media influence myths.

THE WRITING OF MYTH

Herodotus was not a student of written traditions. He was a listener to the tales of great deeds. He spoke no foreign languages and had to rely on informants. He wrote down what he heard and said how intrigued he was by other cultures. He was a writer relying upon nonwriters for his sources. Hence his transcriptions were reenactments of oral traditions about foreign peoples for readers of Greek. Herodotus reacted to his otherness as a writer of tales about others by promoting tolerance and respect for the differences all around him. He trusted his reader to accept the veracity of his writings. His reliance on oral testimony was not, however, popular among his peers. Both Thucydides and Aristophanes criticize the unreliable nature of Herodotus' trust in both his informants and his readers.

Herodotus chose writing as the means to record the myths he heard. Several scholars at the Gernet Center concentrate on the nature of written myth with its writers, readers, and the problems of reading. Jesper Svenbro (Gernet Center), Florence Dupont (University of Paris, IV), and Alain Moreau (University of Montpellier) have been especially influenced in this regard by Gernet's work. Svenbro presents the motto of "J'écris donc je m'efface" ("I write, therefore I erase myself") as the epigraph for his study of the anthropology of reading in ancient Greece, whose title, *Anthropologie de la lecture en Grèce ancienne*, recalls one of Gernet's (*The Anthropology of Ancient Greece*). The reader sustains the textual life of myths after writing erases the writer from interaction with the text. Once written, the writer effectively disappears from the scene and leaves the written document to be deciphered and passed on as the reader finds suitable.

Svenbro recalls the founder of the Phoenician alphabet, Akteon, whose daughter Phoinikè died before him and gave her name to the alphabet. Hence death is part of the heritage of writing. Svenbro also narrates the tale of Phokos, whose daughter Kallirhoè had thirty suitors and thus made the choice so complex that he died before she was betrothed. The father/ daughter relationship is metaphorical for the relationship of writer to the written myth:

> For this relationship of father/daughter, the implication is that the reader assumed the position of the son-in-law. The reader becomes one with the Writing, the daughter of the writer, so that there may be born a legitimate and resounding *logos*.[14]

The *logos* is thus produced by the reader in conjunction

with the text as a "legitimate and resounding" product. Gernet's concern with the legal setting of ancient Greece returns in this "legitimacy," whereby the documentary nature of law is reenacted in a written record. The "resounding" nature mentioned by Svenbro suggests a spiralling return to the oral cultures transcribed by Herodotus because Greek reading was done aloud. Thus Herodotus is the basis for a *logos* both oral and written. It is worth recalling Hartog's note that the authors of the Hellenistic period cited Herodotus to give a realistic impression to their romances. Herodotus is thus part of a written as well as an oral tradition.

The tension between the oral and the written traditions of the *logos* and *muthos* is striking in Plato, the scribe for the spoken dialogues of Socrates and his students. Florence Dupont identifies this tradition as *logos sympotikos* ("the word of the symposium")—the spoken word in the context of the dialogical method.[15] Dupont has been especially influenced by Gernet's studies of Greek and Roman laws. She formulates a "law of the banquet" which links the Greek banquet to the Roman feast. This "law of the banquet" is a way of imposing measure upon the social practice of pleasure. It is not moderation. Rather, it is a means of bringing people together to discuss ideas within the context of pleasure. Dupont identifies this "law" as a "prereferential language"[16] because of the parameters that are thus engaged for the setting in which the dialogues take place. The setting is one for the pursuit of pleasure as a social group at a given place. The consequences are twofold:

> This law of the banquet which legitimizes pleasure acts in two ways: it serves to preclude excess which leads to disgust, and, especially, it allows the construction of cultural delight [*jouissance*] and surpassing pleasure by simple accumulation.[17]

The banquet thus serves as the means to place cultural sanction on desire, thus allowing the participants to master rather than to become victims of infinite desire.

As the instruments of mastering desire, banquets were the settings for the amusement and control of the participants. The place of the banquet was the site for the "construction of cultural delight." Greeks and Romans understood pleasure as a drive that was culturally sanctioned and allied with intellectual activity as well. Hence conversation during the meals and other sensual pastimes was encouraged as part of the cultural goal later celebrated as *mens sana in corpore sano* ("a sound mind in a sound body"). François Lissarrague adds that wine contributed to the banquet: "The idea of sharing that is basic to the Greek use of wine can also be seen in the bond that unites men and gods and that may, or may not, join partners in love."[18]

These pleasures were often conversations that went unrecorded. Likewise there were legends that were not contained by the limits of laws and written documents. Written myths became ways to record the events of the banquets and to establish the limits of the law. Alain Moreau discovers such a myth concerning a banquet given for Oedipus by his son Polynices. This banquet apparently answers the question about why Oedipus is so angry at his sons Eteocles and Polynices that he curses them with internecine wars that eventually destroy the family. The banquet in question involves serving human flesh and blood to Oedipus. Oedipus partakes of the meal and thus adds cannibalism to the list of human taboos of which he is guilty. According to this legend, Polynices collaborates with his brother Eteocles to have Oedipus eat his children by Astymeduse. When Oedipus discovers the nature of his meal, he tips over the table and condemns his sons to mutual warfare and self-destruction. Moreau explains this lost version of Oedipus the cannibal as consistent with Oedipus' known crimes of patricide and incest. The three crimes "appear as the manifestation of an identical principle, violence exerted against that which is similar or rendered similar."[19] The myths of Oedipus are thus presented as tales of assimilation and differentiation linking oral and written versions within the legend of Oedipus.

The Greeks of the city-states linked saying with seeing. Although most myths were *based on* a written text, as with Homer and Hesiod, they were *passed on* by word of mouth. The tale about the cannibalism of Oedipus was apparently prevented from coming down to us by the citizens of Argos, who did not want their native son, Polynices, associated with so heinous a crime. By not allowing this myth of Oedipus to be written down along with the other legends of Oedipus, the elders of Argos hoped to minimize both the ill-effects of the curse of Oedipus and also the reputation of Argos as a cursed place. Moreau begins to look at practices aimed at countering the writing down of Greek myths. The value of writing as a principal conduit of information is thus reinforced by the active effort to prevent the writing of this part of the legend of Oedipus. Writing is also the locus for the struggle in which the written *logos* tests the reliability of the *muthos* from one generation to the next.

THE GREEK EIDETIC IMAGINATION

By translating the stories he heard into written documents, Herodotus provided a model for the visual epistemology of the Greeks. He reproduced the words of an oral testimony. His writing was based on a series of hearings about what someone had seen or had experienced as an original mythical event. Gernet notes that the Greeks were obsessed with visual representations of their myths. This representation of myths through images is the focus of some scholarship by the second-generation Gernet Center scholars. Influenced by the Parisian philosophers Jean-François Lyotard and Jacques Derrida in their explorations of the semiotic relationships between words and images, several scholars associated with the Gernet Center are doing research on the *eidos*, or visual aspect, of classical Greece. François Lissarrague, a researcher at the Centre National pour la Recherche Scientifique, and Jean-Louis Durand, also at the CNRS, have explored the iconography from this period. Françoise Frontisi-Ducroux, of the Collège de France, reveals the Dionysian fixation with masks. The archeologist Alain Schnapp (University of Paris, I) has studied Greek artisans, and Philippe Borgeaud (University of Geneva) has analyzed the festivals of Pan. Frontisi-Ducroux has focused on the feast of Daidala. All of these classicists are fascinated with how the Greek imagination visualized its mythological characters. This visual, or eidetic, quality led to the intersection of the written and visual media and to the creation of plastic arts. While Derrida has been exploring hieroglyphics as a model for writing, his followers note the principle of "ornamentation ... [as] a generative role in text production."[20] What may appear to be marginal or decorative to the words of a myth actually gives clues about the importance of the myth. Lissarrague applies Derrida's theories to study vase painting, where "the letter is a decoration"[21] among the representations of various mythical scenes.

Greek iconography is being developed by the group of scholars inspired by the first generation of Gernet Center. For example, Lissarrague, in Vernant's anthology *La Cité des Images* (1984), incisively links the visual presentation of Greeks to the warrior ethic. He points out the frequent visual depiction of the Athenian citizen taking his place as a warrior to defend the ancestral land. He also isolates the military role of some Greek women, portrayed on vases as carrying the weapons of their men into combat.[22] The glory of the warrior is usually at issue. He is not a member of the hoplite masses. Instead,"the imagists prefer the heroic duel to the ... combat of soldiers in massive engagements."[23]

This "myth" of the Greek soldier as hero is perpetuated through various visual arts, simultaneously reinforcing the positions of Greek men and women. In festivals women were also denied the right to drink wine because of its reputation as the liberating, "nefarious drink."[24] In fact, wine, as a potion usually shared uniquely by men at public events, was often the instigator for homosexual eroticism.[25] The eidetic representation of men and women perpetuates the written codes of behavior placing Greek men and women in apparently unchallenged hierarchical relationships.

At the same time studies of masks reveal a certain playfulness even amidst the rigidity over gender roles. According to Frontisi-Ducroux, the masks are silent and yet have a semiotic message:

> The masks are silent.... What [the mask] has to say to humanity is expressed in the silence of looks and by the sounds which are radically opposed to articulated language: the mysterious moaning of the rhombs in the dionysiac cult, the inhuman groans of the satyrs, the strident yelping of the Gorgons in the mythic narratives, and still everywhere, the uneasy sound of the flute, whose music, so incompatible with the human voice and song, functions as an expression of all that is inexpressible.[26]

Masks were part of the cult of Gorgon (Medusa), Artemis, and Dionysus. Frontisi-Ducroux and Vernant describe Dionysus as "the god of illusions and of continuous confusion between reality and appearances, truth and fiction."[27] Young Spartans used masks in various rituals in order to push the allowable limits of otherness. Through the use of masks the Greeks transgressed social limits and thereby set demarcations for their usual behavior. Women could wear masks of either men or gods and in that guise consume wine destined for men and gods. Frontisi-Ducroux's research recalls the theories of the French intellectual Georges Bataille (1897-1962) about "heteronomy"—a fascination with the other that can make us laugh about ourselves. Frontisi-Ducroux remarks that the Greeks used masks to inspire laughter as a liberating gesture before the serious social constraints of daily living. Men pretended to be gods, beasts, or women. Women pretended to be men or gods. In these ways women and men could create their own myths by acting out their fantasies about having more power in their lives from behind the masks of otherness.

Artisans contributed significantly to the Greek exploration of their otherness. Lissarrague provides one example: "the vase painters are working in a setting in which wine, music, and image are complementary and, on their ties to one another, form a whole web of interrelations; at every level, metaphors and metamorphoses grow under the spell of Dionysus, master of illusion."[28] The masks became crosspoints for this "web of interrelations." Along with the laughter generated by the masks, there was a certain playfulness which the artisan manifested in his/her ambivalent social role: at once remaining in the shadows, condemned for the pursuit of artifice by Plato, while producing the architecture and sculpture of civilization.

Frontisi-Ducroux portrays these paradoxes in a Greek notion, reiterated by the philosopher Martin Heidegger, that "whoever shows and unveils also hides."[29] The Greek artisan was thus an example of *mètis*, or cunning intelligence, whose parameters were developed by Vernant and Detienne. The artisan was so portrayed in the creation of the artistic work known as a *daidalon*—a term applied by Frontisi-Ducroux to encompass all kinds of traps and ruses under the appearances of seduction. Named after Daedalus, a legendary Athenian sculptor and inventor who killed his nephew Perdix for having invented the metal saw and thus showing signs of surpassing his uncle's inventive skills, the artisan's product reflected the Greek respect for ingenuity. Daedalus himself invented the labyrinth for the Minotaur, Ariadne's thread, and the wings to enable himself and his son Icarus to escape imprisonment by Minos. These inventions were the results of his shrewd thinking (*mètis*). Frontisi-Ducroux sees Daedalus as a model for the Greek artisan: "In order to escape the shade, the artisan must be made into a hero of intelligence."[30] "The shade" was not only the threat on the artisan's life but also the social disparagement associated with the choice to "invent" rather than to accept the natural conditions of life. The artifice of the inventor often became art, however, and thus earned the admiration of society.[31]

THE THIRD ORDER

The myths of Greek iconography also evince the role that animals play in stories about gods and humans. Often both gods and humans use animals as mediators in their communications with each other. Philippe Borgeaud describes the revival of the god Pan as an anti-Oedipus: Pan's sexual promiscuity is contrary to the institution of marriage.[32] Part goat and part man, Pan brings the revelry and madness of Arcadia into the mythical constructs of the Greeks. Borgeaud begins his study with a tale from Herodotus about a dream by Philippides that "panic" was invading Persian soldiers on the eve of the Athenian victory at the Battle of Marathon (490 B.C.), the first recorded defeat of the Persians by the Greeks. This "panic" was inspired by the god Pan and became responsible for a widespread cult of the god.

Pan and his joining of divine, human, and animal nature was suggested to Borgeaud by Vidal-Naquet, Detienne, and Loraux. Likewise Vernant and Vidal-Naquet's research into the links among the divine, the human, and the animal in the Greek practices of sacrifice has led research in the fate of the "third order," that of animals. Alain Schnapp, an archaeologist who helped Vidal-Naquet collect the information for the study of the May 1968 revolts in Paris, has studied the iconographic representations of rituals involving animals. Annie Schnapp-Gourbeillon of the University of Caen defended her "thèse de 3e cycle" in 1975 on the study of animals in Greek myths under the direction of Vidal-Naquet and Vernant. Jean-Louis Durand has contributed studies of the iconographic representations of animal physicality.

Detienne speaks of the harmony of the three orders of Greek life. The animal kingdom often comes between humanity and divinity. Animals at once mediate and separate. Gernet himself provided the problem for the second generation mythologists in the Center: "the barrier between human and divine reality: what separates the human from the divine, and, conversely, what brings them together?"[33] In both festivals and myths, as in the personage of Pan, animals so partake of the being of the divinities that Annie Schnapp-Gourbeillon comments that "bestiality and divinity arise from the same inexpressible space."[34] This "inexpressible space" is subject of considerable discussion among the scholars of the Gernet Center.

The example of Pan suggests that the bestial realm is a source of erotic exploration for the gods—a participation in the pleasurable realm of humans. In the pastoral landscapes of

the Arcadian origins of Pan, the hunt of various animals is
synonymous with the divine chasing after bestial company. In
hunting humans imitate gods. Schnapp characterizes the hunt
of the hare as the acting out of adolescent sexual adventure:
"The universe of young people, the ephebic world, thereby
gives a place to physical exercises and athletics, but especially
to seduction, teasing, and to a complex and diversified
eroticism."[35] The eroticism implied in both the divine chase
and the human hunt reflects the common need of both realms
to struggle for control.

Schnapp-Gourbeillon adapts Lévi-Strauss' explanation of
the opposition between nature and culture—in this case the
pastoral versus the urban. Animals represent the struggle
between what is capable of being mastered by society and
what escapes control. Animals thus represent both a frontier
and a gateway.[36] The wild animal lures as a challenge for
control, by both divine and human forces. The domesticated
animal complements and participates in the lives of both.
Schnapp adds that the roles of animals cannot be stereotyped.
His study of the boar hunt, as found in images on the jars and
vases of the period, reveals that the elusive wild animal in the
hunt poses challenges for the ethic of individualism as well as
for the communal responsibility evolving in the city-state.[37]
The hunter demonstrates heroism and cunning in tracking the
boar but also personal responsibility in searching for food for
others. The pursuit of the animal represents both
individualistic and communal values.

Because animals also mediate between gods and humans,
the sacrifice of animals can be either a divine or a human
ritual. The Hesiod's myth of the origin of sacrifice notes that
the gods were tricked into accepting the bones and the innards
of the animals. This event was also the beginning of the eating
of animals by humanity. Jean-Louis Durand notes that the
body of the animal was thus made to disappear. There would
be no trace left of the murder of the animal once thought to be
part of the community of gods and humans. Although much is
said in writings and in iconography about the centrality of the
sacrifice as a reminder of the relationship between the gods
and humanity, Durand explains that the ritual of sacrifice was

invented "so that nothing remains of that about which the text [of sacrifice] is organized, that by which it was produced: the anguish of murder and the horror of spilled blood."[38]

Sacrifice was thus an expiation for hunting. The animal was eradicated as humans felt so heroic that they no longer needed mediators between themselves and the gods. The disappearance of the body of the animal in sacrifice also produced the ambiguous space mentioned by Schnapp-Gourbeillon. Not only was the animal not there, but the humans and the gods no longer had the desire to be either appeased or expiated.

Animals also functioned as mediators *among* humans, not just between humans and gods. Some wild animals ate the flesh of human beings. This animal behavior became paradigmatic of human violence against both animals and other humans. Homer used images of animals to exemplify the savagery of human military battles. As Saïd puts it:

> A human becomes a wolf for another human as is shown by the many images of animals in the act of eating each other or the invocation of vultures and dogs in the act of devouring a cadaver.[39]

Frontisi-Ducroux considers Artemis, "the gatekeeper for the zones of transition and contact as well as the patroness of the passage from savagery to culture,"[40] the protector of this ambiguous boundary between self-preservation and self-destruction. The myth of Acteon is informative. Acteon surprises Artemis while she is bathing. He sees her naked. She transforms him into a stag and has his own dogs devour him. The stag is the transitional animal. Acteon is thus metamorphosed for not knowing his limits as a human. As Acteon surprises the naked goddess, he expresses his human desire and also transgresses the limits of humanity. There are boundaries among the divine, the human, and the animal. Acteon goes too far.

OEDIPUS AND HIS ALTERITY

As the scholars of the Gernet Center explore the roles of animals in Greek myths as both symbols of humans and mediators between humans and gods, they are continuing the research into the awareness of the influence of otherness upon the Greek conception of self. The second generation of Center scholars reinterprets the myth of Oedipus to fit its concern with otherness. The context of the myth is now not only Oedipus' family but also the Greek legal system. Otherness, or "alterity," refers to views of the myth other than the closed triangular relationship of the family and the writing of the myth as tragedy. Gernet's examination of the Greek legal system offers ways to expand reading the Oedipus myth within the context of the law.

The guilt of Oedipus is an intricate legal issue that antedates the writing of the myth as tragedy. Despite being warned about his fate, Oedipus acts in defiance of such advice. Suzanne Saïd believes that, after Oedipus consulted the oracle, he should have avoided both men like his father and women like his mother. She points out that Oedipus is thus guilty even before the action of *Oedipus Rex* begins.[41] In *Oedipus at Colonus* Oedipus denies any fault. Similarly, Antigone portrays herself as the innocent victim of the crimes of her ancestors.[42] These three examples refer to the written tragedies as extrapolations from a story about a judgment already made by others on Oedipus and his family. The intentions and the freedom of Oedipus—the conventional concerns—are not issues. Instead, the legal issue is the responsibility of descendants for the crimes committed by their ancestors. Once again, Saïd finds in Herodotus a key to the principle of *hamartía*, the tragic fault. Herodotus narrates the story of the Lydian pretender Gygès (685-657 B.C.), who killed King Candaules, stole his wife, and then stole his throne to found the Mermnad dynasty. Gygès escaped personal responsibility for restitution through the protection of the Assyrians. Only through his descendant Croesus (550 B.C.) did the Persians achieve retribution for the crimes of Gygès. Analogously, Oedipus and his family suffer for the crimes of

Laius against Pelops. Like the Mermnad dynasty, so the royal line of Cadmus eventually self-destructs.

There is tension between self and otherness—both the otherness of the outsider and that of the differences within a family. Laurence Kahn, one of the members of the second generation of the Gernet Center, stresses the difficulty of communication at the heart of the Oedipus myth[43] as if the silence of others also implies their complicity in the laws that are everywhere surrounding an individual such as Oedipus. Oedipus acts as if he has no knowledge of his father's crime toward Chrysippus, the son of Pelops, and of the laws punishing such crimes. Yet those who judge Oedipus know that there are the laws, even if they are yet explicit. It is only with the Roman Empire that the *logos* so completely overwhelmed *muthos* that the law has to be explicitly written.

The otherness of Oedipus involves not only his marginalization as a pariah in his own kingdom but also his animality explored by the second generation of the Gernet Center. Oedipus' apparent tragic fault is merely an illusion, according to Saïd.[44] The otherness of Oedipus leads to the role of the bestial among humans and gods. Oedipus lacks self-knowledge: he does not know the relative positions of humans, gods, and animals. First, he claims superhuman qualities by not listening to the Delphic oracle. His patricide, incest, and even his purported cannibalism go beyond the limits of natural law, of natural order. His failing stems not from hubris but from ignorance.

Second, Oedipus violates the separation of humans and animals. Laius' horse, on the road to Thebes, is a barrier to Oedipus' ambition. Rather than going around the horse, Oedipus is insulted and slays the driver Laius in anger. The horse represents a frontier for Oedipus. It is both a gateway because Oedipus begins his crimes in the presence of the horse and a frontier because Oedipus does not recognize the space of the animal as a living one to be respected and thus not transgressed. The animal becomes for him a mere object to be overcome by force in his blind trajectory toward self-fulfillment and self-destruction.

The order of animals is crucial in the episode with the

Sphinx. Animals separate rather than symbolize or mediate. Oedipus, who accepts the challenge of the hero capable of defeating the scourge of the city, tests his intellectual ability as a human before this half-animal, half-woman. The Sphinx is his other. She is a cannibal, eating the human flesh of Thebans, thus crossing the line between her and others. Oedipus does not do battle with the Sphinx. Instead, he overwhelms her with human intelligence. The Sphinx then self-destructs. Oedipus does not kill this monster as one would a dragon. Oedipus demonstrates his own talents to do what others could not do: to solve the riddle. But he also shows his potential to cross the line between himself and others, to be better than what other humans have been. Yet in his striving to be other, he inherits Queen Jocasta and ultimately commits the crime of incest, which is the striving toward the self, the struggle between assimilation and differentiation.

As Oedipus constantly pushes the limits beyond his humanity, he also transgresses the boundary between his self and others. Moreau remarks that "among the most primitive customs is the one whereby we eat part or all of another being in order to capture its strength for ourselves."[45] And so it is with Oedipus as he tries to increase his strength by outsmarting both gods and animals. The animals are tests of his character as well as mediators with the gods. They are both tests for the limits of human behavior and extensions of humanity into unknown territory. Oedipus needs the animal realm to realize the full implications of what humanity can and cannot be. Not only human but also divine law governs his behavior. Perhaps even more importantly, natural law reveals itself through the intervention and collaboration of animals with humans and gods.

NOTES

1. For a discussion of the many directions of "new historicism" as well as Greenblatt's alternate term "cultural poetics," see H. Aram Veeser, ed., *The New Historicism* (New York: Routledge, 1989).

2. Louis Gernet, *The Anthropology of Ancient Greece*, trs. John Hamilton and Blaise Nagy (Baltimore: Johns Hopkins University Press, 1981), p. 104.

3. Louis Gernet and André Boulanger, *Le Génie Grec dans la religion* (Paris: Albin Michel, 1932), p. 77.

4. See Stephen Greenblatt, "Toward a Poetics of Culture," in *The New Historicism*, pp. 1-14, for the alternation between "new historicism" and "cultural poetics."

5. Clifford Geertz, *The Interpretation of Cultures* (New York: Basic Books, 1973), chapter 1. The term "thick description" was coined by Gilbert Ryle in his *Concept of Mind* (London: Hutchinson, 1949) but was applied with special cultural insight by Geertz.

6. Hayden White, "New Historicism: A Comment," in *The New Historicism*, p. 293.

7. Cited by François Hartog, *The Mirror of Herodotus: The Representation of the Other in the Writing of History*, tr. Janet Lloyd (Berkeley: University of California Press, 1988), p. xix.

8. Hartog, p. 284.

9. *Ibid.*, p. 192.

10. *Ibid.*, p. 305.

11. Suzanne Saïd and Michèle Rosellini, "Usages de femmes et autres *nomoi* chez les 'sauvages' d'Hérodote: Essai de lecture structurale," *Annali della Scuola Normale Superiore di Pise*, série III, no. 8 (1978), p. 972. All translations from this essay are my own.

12. *Ibid.*, p. 985.

13. Hartog, p. 282 n. 3.

14. Jesper Svenbro, *Phrasikleia: Anthopologie de la lecture en Grèce Ancienne* (Paris: La Découverte, 1988), p. 97. My own translation.

15. Florence Dupont, *Le Plaisir et la loi* (Paris: Maspero, 1977), p. 186. All translations from this book are my own.

16. *Ibid.*, p. 39.

17. *Ibid.*, p. 27.

18. François Lissarrague, *The Aesthetics of the Greek Banquet: Images of Wine and Ritual*, tr. Andrew Szegedy-Maszak (Princeton: Princeton University Press, 1990), p. 86.

19. Alain Moreau, "A propos d'Oedipe: la liaison entre trois crimes—parricide, inceste et cannibalisme," in *Etudes de littérature ancienne*, ed. Suzanne Saïd (Paris: Presses de l'École Normale Supérieure, 1979), p. 114. My own translation.

20. Gregory L. Ulmer, *Applied Grammatology* (Baltimore: Johns Hopkins University Press, 1985), p. 46.

21. Lissarrague, *The Aesthetics of the Greek Banquet*, p. 136.

22. François Lissarrague, "Autour du guerrier," in Jean-Pierre Vernant, ed., *La Cité des images* (Paris: Nathan, 1984), p. 42. All translations from this book are my own.

23. *Ibid.*, p. 40.

24. Jean-Louis Durand, Françoise Frontisi-Ducroux, and François Lissarrague, "L'entre-deux-vins," in *La Cité des images*, p. 120.

25. *Ibid.*, p. 124.

26. Françoise Frontisi-Ducroux, "Au miroir du masque," in *La Cité des images*, p. 159.

27. Françoise Frontisi-Ducroux and Jean-Pierre Vernant, "Figures du masque en Grèce Ancienne," *Journal de psychologie normale et pathologique*, LXXX, 1-2 (1983), p. 68. My own translation.

28. Lissarrague, *The Aesthetics of the Greek Imagination*, p. 143.

29. Françoise Frontisi-Ducroux, *Dédale: Mythologie de l'artisan en Grèce Ancienne* (Paris: Maspero, 1975), p. 191. All translations from this book are my own.

30. *Ibid.*, p. 192.

31. The Daedalus myths continue to be promoted in modern times by the folk dance of Delos, purportedly taught by Daedalus as an imitation of the labyrinth, and by the Feast of Daidala, celebrated in Boetia. These two celebrations are modern testimonies to the survival of Greek myths, in forms other than writing, which continue to respect the artisan's cunning intelligence.

32. Philippe Borgeaud, *The Cult of Pan in Ancient Greece*, trs. Kathleen Atlass and James Redfield (Chicago: University of Chicago Press, 1988), p. 84.

33. Gernet, *The Anthropology of Ancient Greece*, p. 3.

34. Annie Schnapp-Gourbeillon, *Lions, héros, masques: les représentations de l'animal chez Homère* (Paris: Maspero, 1981), p. 203. All translation from this book are my own.

35. Alain Schnapp, "Eros en chasse," in *La Cité des images*, p. 67.

36. Schnapp-Gourbeillon, p. 203.

37. Alain Schnapp, "Images et programme: Les Figurations archaïques de la chasse du sanglier," *Revue archéologique*, II (1979), p. 218. My own translation.

38. Jean-Louis Durand, "Le Corps du délit," *Communications*, No. 26 (1977), p. 59. My own translation.

39. Suzanne Saïd, "Les Crimes des prétendants, la maison d'Ulysse et les festins de l'*Odyssée*," in *Etudes de littérature ancienne*, ed. Saïd (Paris: Ecole de l'école normale supérieure, 1979), p. 27. My own translation.

40. Françoise Frontisi-Ducroux, "L'Homme, le cerf et le berger: chemins grecs de la civilité," *Le Temps de la Réflexion*, IV (1983), p. 55. My own translation.

41. Suzanne Saïd, *La Faute tragique* (Paris: Maspero, 1978), p. 28. All translations from this book are my own.

42. *Ibid.*, p. 129.

43. Laurence Kahn, *Hermès passe ou les ambiguités de la communication* (Paris: Maspero, 1978), p. 185. My own translation.

44. Saïd, *La Faute tragique*, p. 510.

45. Moreau, p. 115.

Conclusion

THE PLACE OF THE GERNET CENTER

The Gernet Center is committed to combining a structural approach to Greek mythology—the approach pioneered by Roland Barthes and especially Claude Lévi-Strauss—with a concern for the distinctively Greek context of that mythology.

Jean-Pierre Vernant says of the importance of the context:

> The aim is to define, as one proceeds, in as exhaustive a fashion as possible, the framework within which the the myth must be set so that every detail in its structure and episodes may take on a precise meaning that can, in every case, be confirmed or refuted by reference to other parts of the body of data as a whole.[1]

For Claude Lévi-Strauss, the context is an ethnographic grid that explains how the lives of the adherents to the myth are reflected in the myth. For Vernant, the context is the social function of myth. Marcel Detienne explains the social functioning of myth in the semantic horizons of the concepts deployed within the story. For Pierre Vidal-Naquet, the context is the intersection of ethics and politics in the myth's recollection of the past. For Nicole

Loraux, the context is the history of the city-state and the psychology of gender. Finally, for the second generation of the Center, the context is the legal otherness found within Greeks myths.

The concern with context has meant that members of the Center have championed philology rather than structural linguistics as the proper way to study language. Structural linguistics, which has influenced non-contextualist structuralists like Barthes and especially Lévi-Strauss, studies language as if changes over time could be ignored. It focuses upon relationships to the exclusion of historical factors. By contrast, philology, by searching for the sources of words, examines how truth evolves over time or how it is disguised by words whose origins are forgotten. These words include terms for crucial concepts like justice, honor, home, right, and balance.

Out of the concerns of philology, the discipline of hermeneutics also arose. Hermeneutics is the study of the process by which symbolic value is given to words. As words develop from other cultures, the new words assume the values of the culture that has invented or borrowed them. Claude Lévi-Strauss and Paul Ricoeur have been arguing for the systematic study of myths either structurally (Lévi-Strauss) or hermeneutically (Ricoeur). The Gernet Center combines the advantages of both perspectives as it investigates the roles played by myth in Greek culture. It operates structurally as it promotes the paradigmatic study of Greek myth and operates hermeneutically by advocating the cultural unity of Greek culture with its myths. Detienne and Vernant, for example, study how cunning intelligence was valued throughout Greek myths. That paradigm was also part of the culture's questioning of the warrior ethic and its representation of its own survival. In this regard Detienne explains Greek myth as "a narrative written from an inquiry into the old and into a past which is not part of history."[2] For him, myth is a written narrative, partly subversive and partly constructive of a cultural identity.

The word "myth" has many conflicting meanings, even for the Greeks. These conflicted meanings are often found in the variances between the structure of the myth and its socio-political basis. Vidal-Naquet, for his part, defines myth as the collective memory of a social group. That memory entails ideologies which are interpretations of historical events that happened to the group. The historian Hayden White notes that because of Vidal-Naquet, it is now recognized that

> an interpretation falls into the category of a lie when it denies the reality of the events of which it treats, and into the category of an untruth when it draws false conclusions from reflection on events whose reality remains attestable on the level of "positive" historical inquiry.[3]

Thus historical inquiry into Greek culture is a continuing part of the research into myths in the Gernet Center.

Detienne finds separate meanings in the word "myth" for Hesiod (the story of human beginnings), Herodotus (an absurd and nonsensical discourse), Aristotle (the plot of a tragedy), and Plato (the derived way of talking about an existing Idea). So there is a need for a frame or a system that allows for the differences in myths across time. Detienne advocates using "mythology" to designate such a system within which individual myths and their theories are bound together. A "mythology" makes connections and creates harmonies among apparently disparate myths. Vidal-Naquet's "black hunter" is thus a mythology uniting the black-cloaked Athenian *ephebe* and the Spartan *kryptoi* with the myths of Melanthos and Melanion. It is a model of the congruency of inside and outside, of the integrity of mythical logic and the correlation with its cultural setting. The issue of correlation has been demonstrated again and again in the structure of *mètis* proposed by Vernant and Detienne, the conditions of death studied by Loraux. The nature of the changes in the relationships between myth and truth is especially exposed in the crucial role that time plays in their various exposés of myths.

PHILOLOGY AND TIME

Philology plays a distinctive role in the research of the Gernet Center. Unlike Lévi-Strauss, who disavows the role of history, Vernant and his colleagues often use the history of a word as the core of their "structural method." The etymons of *mètis*, *daîmon*, *dike*, *pharmakos*, *oikos*, *andreia*, and *arete* reveal information hidden in the merely lexical definition of these terms.

Vidal-Naquet and Florence Dupont reflect two trends in the use of philology. On the one hand Vidal-Naquet's study of "the black hunter" expands the symbolic or hermeneutic range of the adjective "black" far beyond its etymological origins. From the color of young Spartans and Athenians inducted into the larger community, the color then is associated with death. In the myth of Theseus and his father, Aegeus, the mistaken black sail causes the death of Aegeus, himself mistakenly distraught over the death of his son. The color black is also associated with the African race. Black also suggests the night, when special talents like those displayed by the resourceful night fighter are needed. These characteristics of the "black hunter" are best characterized as at once structural—they combine a bundle of meanings gleaned from different symbolic systems—and philological—the words have specific historical settings.

On the other hand Dupont's study of *hamartia* (tragic fault) is more traditional philologically. She traces the evolution of the word *hamartia* to a network of myths underlying tragedies. The "tragic fault" has specific historical purposes within the reworking of myths in tragedy. Philology discovers the specific occurrences of the word *hamartia* and the corresponding sense of responsibility of humanity for its own predicament. Philology thus reveals in the word for "tragic fault" an influence of myth in politics. In the evolution of human government through the city-state, a concomitant development is that the self assumes more responsibility for its mistakes as well as its accomplishments. Myths could be staged and acted out for the Greek populace at large. The development of the city-state eventually devalued the tragic fault along with the sense of guilt associated with myth. Divine intervention gave way to human explanations of tragic situations. Humanity began to accept responsibility for its own destiny by understanding its own mistakes. The eventual abandonment of *hamartia* is a psychological by-product of the transition from *muthos* to *logos*. *Muthos* was part of the human need to find causes for human behavior outside conscious control.

Vernant's philological description of Oedipus' name combines both the structural and the philosophical implications of the contextual method. By combining the etymons *oida* (I know), *pous* (foot), and *oidos* (swollen) to explain the name "Oedipus," Vernant appears to use "folk etymology." However, Vernant has a vision of philology similar to that of Michael Riffaterre for whom the philological goal is "to reconstitute vanished realities."[4] In the case of Oedipus the "vanished reality" is a non-Freudian understanding of Oedipus, whose fate is determined by his swollen foot and his swollen ego. The association of these etymons, not usually brought together to explain Oedipus' name, provides a historical basis for a philosophical inquiry into the ambiguity of the character of Oedipus. Here again, the philological method links the vanished past with the present and becomes a starting point for discussions about the speculative intelligence of the Greeks. Vidal-Naquet's concern with the reassessment of the truth is another testimony to the service that philology plays in the Contextualist method.

PHILOSOPHY AND TIME AND PLACE

Time and place have a special orientation in the Contextualist framework. Ignace Meyerson, the inventor of the term "historical psychology," noted that "the analysis of behavior across historical facts modifies the perspective of the psychological."[5] Likewise for Vernant analysis of the behavior of the Greeks, supplemented by philological facts about key words, modifies the structural perspective of the psychological value of myths. His triangular organization of myth, thought, and society is a statement about the structural connections at the core of Greek culture.

Time is Heidegger's primary criterion for judging the efficacy of human life. He writes about "the coming of the event" (*Ereignis*) as the challenge for individuals to prove their mettle. Similarly, time as *Ereignis* is crucial for the Contextualists. Within myth time provides the opportunity for certain individuals to provide heroic example to a culture and to bring together those virtues admired by that same culture. The coming of the city-state in the sixth century was decisive in the cultural development of Greek antiquity. Myth was involved in the creation of new meaning for human beings who were becoming more confident of their political skills as they formed the city-state. The mettle of the Greeks was formed by their promotion of those political skills that resulted in the formation of collective self-government. Myth served as a way to discuss the nature of those skills by narrating possible scenarios of human self-governance.

The meanings of Greek myths changed as their contexts changed. The event of the city-state was a time that gave tragedy a specifically dramatic context for myth. Vidal-Naquet gives examples of how the change of context affects the reception of myth. He explains how the myth of Alexander the Great during his own lifetime was very different from the myth of Alexander as a model for a king in the seventeenth century.[6] Another example identified by Vidal-Naquet is the myth that war is not a criterion of social organization. This particular myth is disproved by fourth-century Athens when hoplites were used to such an extent that the character of the city became "entirely warlike."[7] Therefore, time is an especially decisive parameter in the determination of the context of myth for the Gernet Center.

Place is likewise a crucial factor in isolating the context for the reception of myth. The otherness of place gives the reader or listener the ability to judge the myth. For the Greeks place had an especially important role in military strategy. Detienne notes the importance of position in discussing the function of the phalanx in Greek combat:

In hoplitic combat, victory doesn't go to the phalanx which has destroyed the largest number of the enemy: it belongs to the party which has pushed back the farthest, which has succeeded in knocking the adversary outside its positions.[8]

The struggle in battle was thus over position. Similarly, the place occupied by each divinity was defined by relative position to another deity. Hermes, for example, represents the open space (*agora*) frequented by men; Hestia, the closed space of the hearth reserved for the married woman.

Loraux shows how the place of women was determined by the denial of their legal staus within the city-state. Since the myth of Pandora represents the first woman as the retribution of Zeus for the trickery of Prometheus, the origin of woman symbolizes the reduction in status of men from *anthropoi* (human beings) to *andres* (males). Women cannot have the same status as men, who once dined with the gods. Greek myth thus provides a philosophical explanation for the enfranchised position by which men distinguished themselves from women. Yet Greek women found their own private place—in their homes, as mothers; in their waiting for men to return from war; and on the stage, where their legal nonplace could be dramatized for all to consider.

REPETITION AT THE CORE

The Contextualists often rework the concepts of their colleagues. *Mètis*, the ambiguity of Oedipus, the *pharmakos*, the three orders, and the hoplites are among the themes that reappear throughout their writings. The Contextualists are not simply copying one another. They are building on one another's work.

What about repetition in myth itself? For Lévi-Strauss, a myth is a synopsis of all the variants. But for the Contextualists, there is no summary version of a myth. At the core of myth is a generalized anecdote which is developed and expanded in many modified versions. In the Oedipus myth, for example, Oedipus is at once savior and assassin, divine king and tyrant, father of the land and worst criminal. For Lévi-Strauss, those opposing qualities are repeated cross-culturally because of the intellectual "human spirit." For the Contextualists these qualities are repeated internally to a culture and interwoven with the specific historical circumstances of the Greek culture. These opposing qualities are repeated not to accentuate the triviality of their opposition. Instead, repetition recurs in a spiralling manner, to hold the the core together and to build on the structural coherence of the myth.

WHAT REALLY HAPPENED

What really happened as the basis for a myth? For Vidal-Naquet the historian, there is a sense of mission at stake in answering this question: "it is the duty of historians to take historical facts out of the hands of ideologists who exploit them."[9] He is ethically committed to separating erroneous information from facts. Presently, he is examining the false, revisionist presentations of the Holocaust by Arthur Butz and Robert Faurisson.

In some way all of the scholars of the Gernet Center are concerned with what really happened. "Really" means something slightly different for each scholar depending where the line is drawn between fiction and verisimilitude. Detienne refers to the congruency between the inside of a myth and its outside. For him, what really happened means that there is a specific historical event that engendered the myth or which the myth subverts. Vernant elaborates the model of a framework. For him, what really happened means the cultural predispositions that subtend and allow the myth to have a social role. Loraux prefers a psychological explanation for the positioning of genders. For her what really happened is a sociological narration of women relative to men. The New Historicists are involved in "thick descriptions." For them, what really happened is a period-specific group of complex forces and relationships that cannot be subsumed under simple theoretical headings such as existential or structuralist.

The Contextualists continue the work outlined by Barthes, who proposed to "unhide" the form of the myths to reveal the ideological alibis and meanings imbedded within the narratives. But unlike both Barthes and Lévi-Strauss, the Contextualists of the Gernet Center refuse to close the myth upon itself. Instead of Lévi-Strauss' dictum that myths think themselves, the Gernet Center scholars assume that myths both reflect and shape the values of those who adhered to them.

NOTES

1. Jean-Pierre Vernant, *Myth and Society in Ancient Greece*, tr. Janet Lloyd (New York: Zone Books, 1988), p. 146.

2. Marcel Detienne, "Le mythe, en plus ou en moins," in Franco Baralla, ed., *Mondo classico: percorsi posibili* (Ravenna: Longo, 1985), p. 26. My translation.

3. Hayden White, *The Content of the Form: Narrative Discourse and Historical Representation*, 2d ed. (Baltimore: Johns Hopkins University Press, 1990), p. 78.

4. Michael Riffaterre, *La Production du texte* (Paris: Seuil, 1979), p. 176.

5. Ignace Meyerson, *Les Fonctions Psychologiques et les oeuvres* (Paris: Vrin, 1948), p. 11. My translation.

6. See Pierre Vidal-Naquet, "Les Alexandres," in Chantal Grell and Christian Michel, eds., *L'Ecole des Princes ou Alexandre Disgracié* (Paris: Les Belles Lettres, 1988), p. 27.

7. Pierre Vidal-Naquet, "La Tradition de l'hoplite athénien," in Jean-Pierre Vernant, ed., *Problèmes de la guerre en Grèce Ancienne* (Paris: Ecole des hautes études en sciences

sociales, 1985), p. 166. My translation.

8. Marcel Detienne, "La Phalange: Problèmes et controverses," in Jean-Pierre Vernant, ed., *Problèmes de la guerre en Grèce Ancienne* (Paris: Ecole des hautes études en sciences sociales, 1985), p. 124. My translation.

9. Pierre Vidal-Naquet, "A Paper Eichmann?", tr. Maria Jolas, *Democracy* I, 2 (Summer 1981), 75.

SELECTED BIBLIOGRAPHY

(1) BY PREDECESSORS OF THE GERNET CENTER

(a) BOOKS

1. GERNET, LOUIS
Anthropologie de la Grèce antique. Paris: Maspero, 1968. *The Anthropology of Ancient Greece*, tr. John Hamilton and Blaise Nagy. Baltimore: Johns Hopkins University Press, 1981.
Les Grecs sans miracle. Ed. Riccardo di Donato. Paris: La Découverte, 1983.

and André Boulanger. *Le Génie grec dans la religion.* Paris: Albin Michel, 1932.

2. MEYERSON, IGNACE
Les Fonctions psychologiques et les oeuvres. Paris: Vrin, 1948.

(b) ARTICLES

1. GERNET
"La Notion mythique de la valeur en Grèce." *Journal de psychologie*, 41 (1948), 415-62. "'Value' in Greek Myth," tr. anonymously. In R.L. Gordon, ed., *Myth Religion & Society* (Cambridge, England: Cambridge University Press, 1981), pp. 111-46.

2. MEYERSON
"L'Oeuvre psychologique de Louis Gernet." In *Hommage à Louis Gernet*, no ed. (Paris: Presses Universitaires de France, 1966), pp. 38-42.

(2) BY THE STRUCTURALISTS

(a) BOOKS

1. BARTHES, ROLAND
Mythologies. Paris: Seuil, 1957. *Mythologies,* tr. Annette Lavers. New York: Hill & Wang, 1972.
Le Plaisir du texte. Paris: Seuil, 1973. *The Pleasure of the Text,* tr. Richard Miller. New York: Hill & Wang, 1975.
Image Music Text, ed. and tr. Stephen Heath. New York: Hill & Wang, 1977.
A Barthes Reader, ed. and tr. Susan Sontag. New York: Hill & Wang, 1982.

2. DETIENNE, MARCEL
La Notion de Daïmôn dans le pythagorisme ancien. Paris: Les Belles Lettres, 1963.
Les Jardins d'Adonis: la mythologie des aromates en Grèce. Paris: Maspero, 1972. *The Gardens of Adonis,* tr. Janet Lloyd with introduction by Jean-Pierre Vernant. Sussex, Eng.: Harvester Press, 1977.
Dionysos mis à mort. Paris: Gallimard, 1977. *Dionysos Slain,* tr. Mireille and Leonard Muellner. Baltimore: Johns Hopkins University Press, 1979.
Les Maîtres de vérité dans la Grèce archaïque. Paris: Maspero, 1979.
L'Invention de la mythologie. Paris: Gallimard, 1981. *The Creation of Mythology,* tr. Margaret Cook. Chicago: University of Chicago Press, 1986.
Dionysos à ciel ouvert. Paris: Hachette, 1986. *Dionysos at Large,* tr. Arthur Goldhammer. Cambridge, MA.: Harvard University Press, 1989.

and Jean-Pierre Vernant. *Les Ruses de l'intelligence: la mètis en Grèce ancienne.* Paris: Flammarion, 1974. *Cunning Intelligence in Greek Culture and Society,* tr. Janet Lloyd. Chicago: University of Chicago Press, 1978.

Edited:
Les Savoirs de l'écriture: en Grèce ancienne. Lille, France: Presses Universitaires de Lille, 1988.

3. DUPONT, FLORENCE
Le Plaisir de la loi. Paris: Maspero, 1977.

4. FRONTISI-DUCROUX, FRANÇOISE
Dédale, mythologie de l'artisan. Paris: Maspero, 1975.

5. HARTOG, FRANÇOIS
Le Miroir d'Hérodote. Paris: Gallimard, 1980. *The Mirror of Herodotus: The Representation of the Other in the Writing of History,* tr. Janet Lloyd. Berkeley: University of California Press, 1988.

6. KAHN, LAURENCE
Hermès passe ou les ambiguités de la communication. Paris: Maspero, 1978.

7. LÉVI-STRAUSS, CLAUDE
Anthropologie structurale. Paris: Plon, 1958. *Structural Anthropology.* Vol. I, trs. Claire Jacobson and Brooke G. Schoepfe. New York: Basic Books, 1963. *Structural Anthropology II,* tr. Monique Layton. Chicago: University of Chicago Press, 1976.
La Pensée sauvage. Paris: Plon, 1962. *The Savage Mind,* tr. anonymously. Chicago: University of Chicago Press, 1966.
Le Totemisme aujourd'hui. Paris: Presses Universitaires de France, 1962. *Totemism,* tr. Rodney Needham. Boston: Beacon Press, 1963.
Mythologiques. Vol. I - IV, trs. John and Doreen Weightman. Vol. I: *Le Cru et le cuit.* Paris: Plon, 1964. *The Raw and the Cooked.* New York: Harper & Row, 1969. Vol. II: *Du Miel aux cendres.* Paris: Plon, 1966. *From Honey to Ashes.* Chicago: University of Chicago Press, 1973. Vol. III: *De l'Origine des manières de table.* Paris: Plon, 1968. *The Origin of Table Manners.* New York: Harper & Row, 1978. Vol. IV:

L'Homme nu. Paris: Plon, 1971. *The Naked Man.* New York: Harper & Row, 1981.
Myth and Meaning. New York: Shocken, 1979.

and Didier Eribon, *De Près et de loin.* Paris: Odile Jacob, 1988.

8. LISSARRAGUE, FRANÇOIS
Un Flot d'images: une esthétique du banquet grec. Paris: Adam Biro, 1987. *The Aesthetics of the Greek Banquet: Images of Wine and Ritual,* tr. Andrew Szegedy-Maszak. Princeton: Princeton University Press, 1990.

9. LORAUX, NICOLE
L'Invention d'Athènes: histoire de l'oraison funèbre dans la 'cité classique.' Paris: Editions de l'Ecole des Hautes Études en Sciences Sociales, 1981. *The Invention of Athens: The Funeral Oration in the Classical City,* tr. Alan Sheridan. Cambridge, MA.: Harvard University Press,1986.
Les Enfants d'Athéna: idées athéniennes sur la citoyenneté et la division des sexes. Paris: La Découverte, 1984.
Les Façons traqigues de tuer une femme. Paris: Hachette, 1985. *Tragic Ways of Killing a Woman,* tr. Anthony Forster. Cambridge, MA.: Harvard University Press, 1987.

10. SAÏD, SUZANNE
La Faute tragique. Paris: Maspero, 1978.

Edited:
Études de littérature ancienne. Paris: Presses de l'Ecole Normale Supérieure, 1979.

11. SCHNAPP-GOURBEILLON, ANNIE
Lions, héros, masques: les représentations de l'animal chez Homère. Paris: Maspero, 1981.

12. SVENBRO, JESPER

La Parole et le marbre: aux origines de la poétique grecque.
Lund, Sweden: Studentlitteratur, 1976.
Phrasikleia: anthropologie de la lecture en Grèce ancienne.
Paris: La Découverte, 1988.

13. VERNANT, JEAN-PIERRE

Les Origines de la pensée grecque. Paris: Presses
Universitaires de France, 1962. *The Origins of Greek
Thought,* tr. anonymously. Ithaca, N.Y.: Cornell University
Press, 1982.
Mythe et pensée chez les Grecs. Paris: Maspero, 1965. *Myth and
Thought among the Greeks,* tr. anonymously. London:
Routledge & Kegan Paul, 1983.
Mythe et société en Grèce ancienne. Paris: Maspero, 1974. *Myth
and Society in Ancient Greece,* tr. Janet Lloyd. New York:
Zone, 1988.
Mortals and Immortals: Collected Essays, tr. Froma I.Zeitlin.
Princeton: Princeton University Press, 1991.

and Marcel Detienne. *Les Ruses de l'intelligence: la métis des
Grecs.* Paris: Maspero, 1974. *Cunning Intelligence in Greek
Culture and Society,* tr. Janet Lloyd. Atlantic Highlands,
N.J.: Harvester Press, 1978.
and Marcel Detienne. *La Cuisine du sacrifice en pays grec.*
Paris: Gallimard, 1979. *The Cuisine of Sacrifice among the
Greeks,* tr. Paula Wissing. Chicago: University of Chicago
Press, 1989.
and Pierre Vidal-Naquet. *Mythe et tragédie en Grèce
ancienne.* Vol. I. Paris: Maspero, 1972. Vol. II: Paris: La
Découverte, 1986. Combined as *Myth and Tragedy in
Ancient Greece,* tr. Janet Lloyd. Sussex, Eng.: Harvester
Press, 1981. Reprint, New York: Zone, 1988.

Edited:
Problèmes de la guerre en Grèce ancienne. Paris: Ecole Pratique
des Hautes Études, 1968. Reprint, Ecole des Hautes Études
en Sciences Sociales, 1985.

La Cité des Images: L'iconographie et la société en Grèce ancienne. Paris: Nathan, 1984. *A City of Images: Iconography and Society in Ancient Greece,* tr. Deborah Lyons. Princeton: Princeton University Press, 1989.

14. VIDAL-NAQUET, PIERRE
L'Affaire Audin. Paris: Minuit, 1958.
La Torture dans la république. Paris: Minuit, 1972. *Torture: Cancer of Democracy,* tr. Barry Richard. Baltimore: Penguin, 1963.
Les Crimes de l'armée française. Paris: Maspero, 1975.
Les Juifs, la mémoire et le présent. Vol. I, Paris: Maspero, 1981. Vol. II, Paris: La Découverte, 1991.
Le Chasseur noir: formes de pensée et formes de société dans le monde grec. Paris: Maspero, 1981. Reprint. La Découverte, 1983. *The Black Hunter: Forms of Thought and Forms of Society in the Greek World,* tr. Andrew Szegedt-Maszak. Baltimore: Johns Hopkins University Press, 1986.

Les Assassins de la mémoire. Paris: La Découverte, 1987.

Edited:
La Raison d'état: textes publiés par le Comité Maurice Audin. Paris: Minuit, 1962.
and Pierre Lévêque. *Clisthène l'athénien.* Paris: Belles Lettres, 1964.
and Michel Austin. *Economie et société en Grèce ancienne.* Paris: Colin, 1972. *Economic and Social History of Ancient Greece: An Introduction,* tr. Michel Austin. Berkeley: University of California Press, 1977.
and Alain Schnapp. *Journal de la commune étudiante: de novembre 1967 à juin 1968.* Paris: Seuil, 1969. *French Student Uprising: November 1967-June 1968,* tr. Maria Jolas. Boston: Beacon, 1977.
and Jean-Pierre Vernant. *Oedipe et ses mythes.* Paris: Editions Complexe, 1988.

(b) ANTHOLOGIES OF THE GERNET SCHOOL
Vidal-Naquet, Pierre, ed. *Aristophane, les Femmes et la Cité.*
Paris: Cahiers de Fontenay, 1979.
Gordon, R.L., ed. and tr. *Myth, Religion and Society:
Structuralist Essays by Detienne, Gernet, Vernant and
Vidal-Naquet.* Cambridge, U.K.: Cambridge University
Press, 1981.
Izard, Michael and Pierre Smith, eds., *Between Belief and
Transgression: Structuralist Essays on Religion, History, and
Myth.* Chicago: University of Chicago Press, 1982. Vernant,
Jean-Pierre, ed. *La Cité des images.* Paris: Nathan, 1984.
Du châtiment dans la cité, anonymously edited. Rome: Ecole
française de Rome, 1984.
Vernant, Jean-Pierre. *Problèmes de la guerre en Grèce
ancienne.* Paris: Ecole des études en sciences sociales, 1985.

(c) ESSAYS AND ARTICLES

1. BARTHES, ROLAND
"France: Mère des Arts?" *Les Lettres Nouvelles,* February
1963, pp. 71-80.
"Du mythe à l'écriture." Preface to LaBruyère, *Les
Caractères.* Paris: 10/18, 1963, pp. 5-23.
"L'Ancienne Rhétorique." *Communication,* No. 16 (1970),
pp. 172-237.
"Par où commencer?" *Poétique,* 1 (Spring 1970), pp. 3-9.
"En Marge du Criton." *L'Arc,* No. 56 (1974), pp. 4-7.

2. DETIENNE, MARCEL
"Entre bêtes et dieux." *Nouvelle revue de psychanalyse,* 6
(Autumn 1972), 231-246. "Between Beasts and Gods," trs.
Maria Jolas and Pierre Vidal-Naquet. In R. L. Gordon, ed.,
Myth Religion and Society. Cambridge, U.K.: Cambridge
University Press, 1981, pp. 215-228.
"Potagerie de femmes ou comment engendrer seule."
Traverses, 5-6 (1976), pp. 75-81.
"Au commencement était le corps des dieux." *Critique,* 34
(November 1978), pp. 1043-1056.

"Repenser la mythologie." In Michel Izard and Pierre Smith, eds., *La Fonction symbolique* (Paris: Gallimard, 1979), pp. 71-82. "Rethinking Mythology," tr. John Leavitt. In Michel Izard and Pierre Smith, ed., *Between Belief and Transgression: Structuralist Essays on Religion, History, and Myth* (Chicago: University of Chicago Press, 1982), pp. 43-52.

"Le Mythe en plus ou en moins." In *Mondo classico: percorsi possibili*, ed. Franco Baralla et al. (Ravenna: Longo, 1985), pp. 11-26.

"Du Polythéisme en général." *Classical Philology*, 81 (January 1986), pp. 47-55.

"L'Apollon meurtrier et les crimes de sang." *Quaderni urbinati di cultura classica*, 51 (1986), 7-17. "Apollo's Slaughterhouse," tr. Anne Doueihi, *Diacritics*, 16 (Summer 1986), pp. 46-53.

"Dionysos en ses parousies: un dieu épidémique." In *L'Association dionysiaque dans les sociétés anciennes*, ed. anonymously (Rome: Ecole française de Rome, 1986), pp. 53-83.

"L'Ecriture et ses nouveaux objets intellectuels en Grèce." *Mètis: Revue d'anthopologie du monde grec ancien*, 1 (Spring 1986), pp. 309-324.

3. DUPONT, FLORENCE

"La Scène juridique." *Communications*, No. 26 (1977), pp. 62-77.

4. DURAND, JEAN-LOUIS

"Le Corps du délit." *Communications*, No. 26 (1977), pp. 46-61.

5. FRONTISI-DUCROUX, FRANÇOISE

"L'Homme, le cerf et le berger." *Le Temps de la réflexion*, 4 (1983), pp. 53-76.

and Jean-Pierre Vernant. "Figures du masque en Grèce ancienne." *Journal de psychologie normale et pathologique*, 80, No. 1-2 (Spring 1983), pp. 53-69.

6. LÉVI-STRAUSS, CLAUDE

"La Structure des mythes." *Journal of American Folklore*, LXXVIII (October 1955), pp. 428-444. Also in Lévi-Strauss, *Anthropologie structurale*, vol. I. Paris: Plon, 1958, pp. 227-256. "The Structural Study of Myth," trs. Claire Jacobson and Brooke Schoepf. In Lévi-Strauss, *Structural Anthropology* (New York: Basic Books, 1963), pp. 206-231.

"La Geste d'Asdiwal," *Annuaire 1958-1959, Ecole pratique des hautes études*, Section des sciences sociales (Paris: 1958), pp. 3-43. "The Story of Asdiwal," trs. N. Mann and Monique Layton. In Lévi-Strauss, *Structural Anthropology II*, tr. Monique Layton (Chicago: University of Chicago Press, 1976), pp. 146-197.

and Roman Jakobson. "'Les Chats' de Charles Baudelaire," *L'Homme*, 2 (January-April 1962), 5-21. "Charles Baudelaire's 'Les Chats,'" tr. Fernande de George. In Richard and Fernande de George, *The Structuralists from Marx to Lévi-Strauss* (Garden City, N.Y.: Anchor Books, 1972), pp. 124-146.

7. LORAUX, NICOLE

"Deux versions de la mort du combattant athénien." *Ancient Society*, 6 (1975), pp. 1-31.

"La 'belle mort' spartiate," *Ktema*, 2 (1977), pp. 105-120.

"Mourir devant Troie, tomber pour Athènes: De la gloire du héros à l'idée de la cité." *Social Science Information*, 17 (1978), pp. 801-817.

"Sur la race des femmes et quelques-unes de ses tribus." *Arethusa*, 11 (1978), pp. 43-87.

"Thucydide n'est pas un collègue." *Quaderni di storia*, 12 (July-December 1980), pp. 55-81.

"Le Lit, la guerre." *L'Homme*, 21 (January-March 1981), pp. 37-67.

"Héraklès: le surmâle et le féminin." *Revue française de psychanalyse*, 46 (1982), pp. 607-729.

"Le Corps étranglé: quelques faits et beaucoup de représentations." In *Du Châtiment dans la cité*, ed.

anonymously (Rome: Ecole française de Rome, 1984), pp. 195-224.

"Socrate, Platon, Héraklès: sur un paradigme héroïque du philosophe." In Jacques Brunschwig, ed. *Histoire et structure* (Paris: Vrin, 1985), pp. 94 ff.

8. SAÏD, SUZANNE

"Les Crimes des prétendants, la maison d'Ulysse et les festins de l'*Odyssée*." In Saïd, ed., *Etudes de littérature ancienne* (Paris: Presses de l'Ecole Normale Supérieure, 1979), pp. 9-49.

and Michelle Rossellini. "Usages des femmes et autres *nomoi* chez les 'sauvages' d'Hérodote: Essai de lecture structurale." *Annali della Scuola Normale Superiore di Pise*, 3, No. 8 (1978), pp. 949-1005.

9. SCHNAPP, ALAIN

"Images et programme: les figurations archaïques de la chasse du sanglier." *Revue archéologique*, 2 (Summer 1979), pp. 195-218.

10. VERNANT, JEAN-PIERRE

"Ambiguity and Reversal: On the Enigmatic Structure of *Oedipus Rex*," tr. Page duBois, *New Literary History*, 9 (1977-8), pp. 475-501.

"Manger au pays du Soleil." In *Culture Science et développement: Mélanges en l'honneur de Charles Morazé*, ed. anonymously (Toulouse: Privat, 1979), pp. 59-63.

"La Belle Mort et le cadavre outragé." In Vernant and Gherardo Gnoli, eds., *La Mort, les morts dans les sociétés anciennes* (Cambridge, U.K.: Cambridge University Press, 1982), pp. 45-76.

"Feminine Figures of Death in Greece," tr. Anne Doueihi, *Diacritics*, 16 (Summer 1986), pp. 54-64.

11. VIDAL-NAQUET, PIERRE

"Temps des dieux et temps des hommes." *Revue de l'histoire des religions*, 157 (January 1960), pp. 55-80.

"Bêtes, hommes et dieux chez les Grecs." In Leon Poliakov, ed., *Hommes et bêtes: Entretiens sur le racisme* (Paris: Mouton, 1975), pp. 130-9.

"Oedipe à Vicence et à Paris: deux moments d'une histoire." In *Quaderni di storia* (Spring 1975), pp. 3-29.

"Plato's Myth of the Statesman, the Ambiguities of the Golden Age and of History," tr. Maria Jolas, *Journal of Hellenic Studies*, 98 (1978), pp. 132-41.

"A Paper Eichmann?", tr. Maria Jolas, *Democracy*, 1 (Spring 1981), pp. 70-95.

"Dreyfus dans l'Affaire et dans l'histoire." Introd. to Alfred Dreyfus, *Cinq Années de ma vie (1894-1899)* (Paris: Maspero, 1982), pp. 1-48.

"De l'erreur judiciaire au crime judiciaire." Afterword to Gisèle Tichané, *Coupable à tout prix—L'Affaire Luc Tangorre* (Paris: La Découverte, 1984), pp. 193-208.

"The Black Hunter Revisited." *Proceedings of the Cambridge Philological Society*, 32 (Spring 1986), pp. 126-144.

"Oedipe entre deux cités: essai sur *l'Oedipe à Colone*." *Mètis: Revue d'anthopologie du monde grec ancien*, 1 (Spring 1986), pp. 37-69.

"Les Alexandres." In Chantal Grell and Christian Michel, eds., *L'Ecole des princes ou Alexandre disgracié* (Paris: Les Belles Lettres, 1988), pp. 5-27.

"Pour un ami disparu: hommage à Marcel Liebman." *Revue d'Etudes palestiniennes*, 30 (Winter 1989), pp. 101-108.

and Jacques Le Goff, "Lévi-Strauss en Brocéliande." In Raymond Bellour and Catherine Clément, eds., *Claude Lévi-Strauss* (Paris: Gallimard, 1979), pp. 267-319.

See also the critical bibliography of Vidal-Naquet by Pierre Pachet, "Pierre Vidal-Naquet: Jeunesse et Tradition," *Critique*, 38 (March 1982), pp. 224-230.

(3) ABOUT THE PREDECESSORS OF THE GERNET SCHOOL STRUCTURALISTS

(a) BOOKS

Barbu, Zevedei. *Problems of Historical Psychology.* New York: Grove Press, 1960.

Hommage à Louis Gernet, ed. anonymously. Paris: Presse Universitaires de France, 1966.

(b) ARTICLE
Di Donato, Riccardo. "Une Oeuvre, un itinéraire." In Louis Gernet, *Les Grecs sans miracle*, ed. Di Donato (Paris: La Découverte, 1983), pp. 403-420.

(4) ABOUT THE GERNET SCHOOL STRUCTURALISTS

(a) REVIEWS OF THEIR BOOKS
1. Review of Vernant, *Mythe et pensée chez les Grecs*:

Delfradas, J. "Le Mythe hésiodique des races." *L'Information littéraire*, 4 (1965), pp. 152-156.

2. Review of Vernant and Vidal-Naquet, *Mythe et tragégie en Grèce ancienne*:

Loraux, Nicole. "L'Interférence tragique." *Critique*, 29 (October 1973), pp. 908-925.

3. Review of Vidal-Naquet, *Le Chasseur noir*:

Knox, Bernard. "Greece à la française." *New York Review of Books*, 30 (3 March 1983), pp. 26-30.

4. Review of Vidal-Naquet, *Les Juifs, la mémoire et le présent* and *Le Chasseur noir*:

Pachet, Pierre. "Pierre Vidal-Naquet: Jeunesse et Tradition." *Critique*, 38 (March 1982), pp. 213-230.

5. Review of Vidal-Naquet, *Les Juifs, la mémoire et le présent*, volume 2:

Jacques-Emile Miriel, "L'immense palais de la mémoire," *Magazine littéraire*, No. 293 (November 1991), p. 89.

6. Review of Vernant, *Mythe et pensée chez les Grecs* and Detienne's *L'Invention de la mythologie*:

diPiero, Thomas. "A Myth is as Good as a Smile." *Diacritics*, 16 (Summer 1986), pp. 21-33.

7. Review of Detienne, *Les Maîtres de Vérité dans la Grèce ancienne* and Vernant and Detienne, *Cunning Intelligence in Greek Culture and Society*:

Harrison, Robert Pogue. "The Ambiguities of Philology," *Diacritics*, 16 (Summer 1986), pp. 14-20.

8. Review of Detienne and Vernant's *Les Ruses de l'intelligence*:

Klein, Richard. "The Mètis of Centaurs." *Diacritics*, 16 (Summer 1986), pp. 2-13.

9. Review of Detienne's *The Creation of Mythology*:

Segal, Robert. *Journal of the American Academy of Religion*, 56 (Spring 1988), pp. 147-149.

(b) BOOKS ON THE STRUCTURALISTS

Picard, Raymond. *Nouvelle critique ou nouvelle imposture?* Utrecht: Pauvert, 1965. *New Criticism or New Fraud?*, tr. Frank Towne. Pullman, WA.: Washington State University Press, 1969.

Ricoeur, Paul. *Le Conflit des interprétations: Essais d'herméneutique.* Paris: Seuil, 1969. *The Conflict of Interpretations*, tr. Don Ihde. Evanston, IL.: Northwestern University Press, 1974.

Mounin, Georges. *Introduction à la sémiologie.* Paris: Minuit, 1970.

Macksey, Richard and Eugenio Donato, ed. *The Structuralist Controversy: The Languages of Criticism and the Sciences of Man.* Baltimore: Johns Hopkins University Press, 1972.

Glucksmann, Miriam. *Structuralist Analysis in Contemporary Social Thought.* London: Routledge and Kegan Paul, 1974.

Culler, Jonathan. *Structuralist Poetics.* Ithaca, N.Y.: Cornell University Press, 1975.

Champagne, Roland A. *Beyond the Structuralist Myth of Ecriture.* The Hague: Mouton, 1977.

Pettit, Philip. *The Concept of Structuralism: A Critical Analysis.* Berkeley: University of California Press, 1977.

Johnson, Barbara. *The Critical Difference.* Baltimore: Johns Hopkins University Press, 1980.

Kurzweil, Edith. *The Age of Structuralism.* New York: Columbia University Press, 1980.

Di Benedetto, Vincenzo, and Alesandro Lami. *Filologia e marxismo—Contra le mistificazioni.* Naples: Liguori, 1981.

Lemert, Charles C. and Garth Gillian. *Michel Foucault: Social Theory and Transgression.* New York: Columbia University Press, 1982.

Champagne, Roland A. *Literary History in the Wake of Roland Barthes.* Birmingham, AL.: Summa Publications, 1984.

Smith, Steven B. *Reading Althusser.* Ithaca, N.Y.: Cornell University Press, 1984.

Duchen, Claire. *Feminism in France: May '68 to Mitterand.* London: Routledge and Kegan Paul, 1986.

Roger, Philippe. *Roland Barthes, Roman.* Paris: Grasset et Fasquelle, 1986.

Champagne, Roland A. *Claude Lévi-Strauss.* Boston: Twayne, 1987.

White, Hayden. *The Content of the Form: Narrative Discourse and Historical Representation,* 2d ed. Baltimore: Johns Hopkins University Press, 1989 [1987].

Champagne, Roland A. *French Structuralism.* Boston: Twayne World Author Series, 1990.

(c) JOURNAL ISSUES ON THE GERNET SCHOOL

Arethusa, 15 (Spring 1982). American Classical Studies Association special issue in honor of Jean-Pierre Vernant.

Diacritics, 16 (Summer 1986), ed. Milad Doueihi. Special issue on "The Mètis of the Greeks."

INDEX

Vidal-Naquet, Pierre, 2, 3,
    6, 12, 15, 16, 17, 26,
    38, 61, 69, 70, 83, 107,
    113-38, 140, 147, 153,
    161, 163, 167, 175,
    185, 187, 189, 190, 192
Voltaire (François-Marie
    Arouet), 165

warrior, 78, 79, 117, 127,
    130, 140, 142, 143,
    144, 172
White, Hayden, 163, 187
wife, 35, 38, 92, 127
wine, 89, 170, 172
women, 6, 7, 9, 10, 15, 16,
    36, 38, 39, 65, 70-2,
    78, 79, 82-3, 86, 92,
    93, 97, 98, 104, 105,
    106, 125-7, 131, 140-
    59, 166, 167, 172, 173,
    186, 191, 192
writing, 3, 10, 14, 15, 29,
    59, 61, 70, 87, 91, 92,
    96, 139, 164, 167-71,
    172, 178, 186, 191

Xanthos, 129
Xenophanes, of Colophon,
    95

Yvain, 117

Zauces, 166
Zeus, 35, 41, 70, 75, 78,
    90, 96, 104, 126, 152,
    191